CHANNELLING

CHANNELLING

USE YOUR PSYCHIC POWERS TO
CONTACT YOUR SPIRIT GUIDES

Shirley Humphreys Battie

A GODSFIELD BOOK
www.godsfieldpress.com

First published in Great Britain in 2006
by Godsfield Press,
a division of Octopus Publishing Group Ltd
2–4 Heron Quays,
London E14 4JP

Distributed in the United States and Canada by
Sterling Publishing Co., Inc.
387 Park Avenue South, New York, NY 10016–8810

ISBN-13: 978-1-84181-291-5
ISBN-10: 1-84181-291-9

A CIP catalogue record for this book is available from the British Library.

1 3 5 7 9 10 8 6 4 2

Printed and bound in China

Contents

Introduction

Channelling is easy for most people. It is not necessary to be psychic from birth to have conversations with spirit minds. You may have surprised yourself by saying something without thinking first, and what you have said proved to be wise and helpful. You may have wondered why you said what you did, when you had no intention of speaking at all. Where did this information and wisdom come from? Perhaps you channelled it by tapping into the field of consciousness that surrounds you and expressed the message in words.

The ability to channel from your inner self and greater consciousness is available to anyone who wishes to make use of this help. You have the ability to channel, if you want to. It is the aim of this book to show you how to go into a trance. In a trance, your consciousness is expanded and inner senses heightened so that you are fine-tuned to messages from the world of spirit. You will learn to see, hear and sense with your mind and vocally express what you receive.

Channelling is not new. Many prophets of the world's faiths spoke channelled words, and many inventions and discoveries came about through individuals entering a light trance or dream state and bringing back solutions to a problem. It is often said that our greatest composers and artists were inspired. You too can be inspired.

Many spirit forms and angels have no specific gender one way or the other. Therefore throughout the book, to avoid confusion and to make for easier reading, guides, angels and other spirit beings are always referred to in the masculine, although they can be of masculine or feminine gender, or neither.

What is channelling?

The word 'channelling' means to pass a substance through a conduit from one area to another. A substance can mean many things, physical or non-physical. When we refer to spiritual or psychic matters, it means channelling energy and/or intelligence from a source invisible to the human eye. A channeller is one who acts as that conduit and is often referred to as a Vehicle or Instrument. A person can channel knowingly and with intent, or subconsciously. A natural healer, who is quite aware of the ability to call on Higher Forces for healing work, is able to interact with greater minds for information and techniques that will assist in the healing process. To do this the healer enters a light meditative state of mind to channel and make use of the healing energy.

Another use of channelling is to put forward ideas, ideals and information covering many fields of interest, spiritual

values, visual images and love. You, and you alone, decide what it is you allow to be channelled through you. You needn't restrict yourself to one thing.

To channel with intent is to operate as the conduit for the purpose of connecting the Higher Realms of consciousness with the third-dimensional mind. In order to do this you go into an expanded state of being through meditation, which brings your soul, guides or teachers to you. These beings are able to access the much Higher Realms of consciousness and act as a bridge, thereby bringing to you and others a wider knowledge and understanding of the deeper meanings of life.

Your guides assist you with their energy and encouragement. They teach you to be discerning in what and whom you accept or discard, when receiving from a non-physical source.

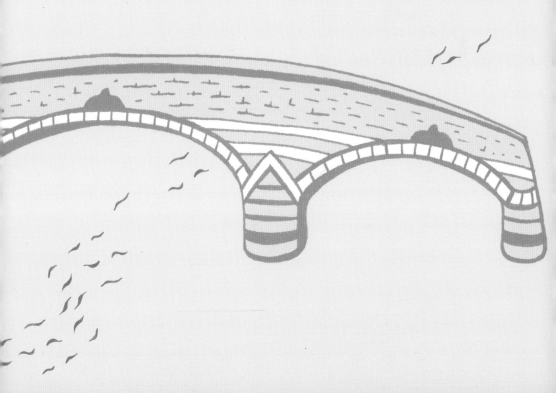

They show you spiritual values and the advantages they may bring. They teach you responsibility for your thoughts and actions. They may make suggestions for your progress along your chosen path.

It is often said that your guides are aspects of self. If you consider that we are all united as one great consciousness, then this is true. What you receive through channelling may give you the 'I know this already' feeling. Do not discard what you hear because of this, since this is proof that we are all linked with the great subconscious and that you have simply tapped into this resource.

However, it is important to remember that you need to have control over and responsibility for what is passed through you as a channel. You will be shown how to recognize the difference between playful spirits and those who have something of value to give through you.

As your soul expands in understanding and your level of vibration is raised to even greater heights, you will not need the assistance of the guides to act as a go-between in your channelling. You will have a direct line to the Masters and the Angelic Realm. Your own level of vibration will raise you to closer and easier connection with the Spiritual Realms as you continue to be a channel for good.

A PERSONAL ACCOUNT

You might be wondering how I started channelling. As a mother and grandmother I had no interest in psychic or spiritual matters while surviving two stressful marriages. While working and living in Italy I held discussion groups on such matters as life after death and psychic spiritual connections. I had no thought that I would actively engage in this work. Returning to England from France in 1990, I meditated for the first time and had instant connection with spirit guides. 'You no longer have family commitments,' they told me. 'We have been waiting.' My family are still trying to understand me but are doing well so far.

My guides showed me many scenes concerning the future of the planet. That got my attention. They taught me how to record their communications, which led to light trance channelling. They have helped me to raise my vibrations, which have felt quite physical at times. While in France I was called 'Chouette', which is French for Little Owl. It seemed an appropriate name to adopt since I do not regard myself as a wise old owl but as a fledgling owl that is still learning.

My connection with a spirit world is cosmic and includes our Space Brothers and The White Brotherhood. Inspirational messages from them have been collected into a pack of Little Owl Cards. The messages are still coming.

Since I made contact my life has been enormously happy and fulfilling. It has taken me all over the world and I have met wonderful people everywhere. If I can help you to make the same contact I certainly will.

Why learn to channel?

Imagine you have a friend who is always available to help you with life's problems and, more excitingly, could clear up some of the mysteries of existence. Wouldn't you really want to be with him? Of course you would.

When you channel you have access to all the help and information you will ever need for your own spiritual growth and for enlightenment on so many subjects. The trick is to ask questions, either in your own mind or by getting others to ask them. In the latter case, it is helpful if they are present in the room with you and adding their energies. Providing you ask questions you will certainly get answers.

You will draw to you guides who have the same field of interest as yourself and who will provide you with a greater understanding of the world in which you live. You will draw to you one who speaks your language so that you can relate

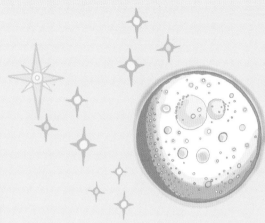

to each other well. If, for example, your interest is in ecology, then the information that comes through you will be along those lines. If, on the other hand, your interest is in understanding the minds of others so that you could help them, you will draw to you one who is qualified to speak on those matters. In this way you will always be comfortable in your connection with him.

Guides are happy when they are able to work with a channeller who is already enlightened regarding their field of expertise. If your interests are in tune, then you will be drawn to them and they to you.

LEARN WHAT HAPPENS AFTER DEATH

One of the questions that many wish to know the answer to is where we go after we die. It is an understandable concern. The guide who is speaking almost certainly has had lives on Earth and clearly is most qualified to give you the answer to that question. He will tell you that life goes on. Depending on how you ask your questions, he will give examples of what happens during your transition and afterwards.

You will discover through your guide how the spirit world views suicides, or about what happns when a soul enters the body after conception. You may ask about traumatic or sudden death when no preparation has been possible. You may be told that learning does not stop with death. Often spirit existence is busier and more exciting than life in a body on Earth. You will learn that even after many years a love connection does not break with death and that many loved ones surround you when you arrive in the spirit world.

You will be told that living in the spirit world is not so very different from a physical life, but without the restrictions of a physical body. Depending on the circumstances of death, some take a while to realize that they are no longer alive in a physical sense. They will be helped to adjust to their new environment. Nobody is left to deal with the transfer alone, unless they wish it.

Asking questions is important. As it says in the Bible: 'Ask and you shall receive: Seek and you shall find.'

Often a channelled guide will know what is in your mind, or the minds of others present, without it being expressed. He may supply answers to after-life questions during a discourse. This is often surprising to many, but proves without doubt that the spirit world is indeed connecting with you.

MEET YOUR GUIDES AND TEACHERS

Have you ever wondered why the guides often present themselves as coming from ancient civilizations? The thing to

remember is that they can and do present themselves to your mind in any way they choose. Many choose to show themselves as Indian, Chinese, Aboriginal, Greek, Middle Eastern, Native American and so on. In this way they make you sit up and take notice. It is not that a modern-looking man in a suit could not turn up or would not have anything of importance to impart, but how much impact would he have on you?

A guide may have had a past-life connection with you, especially if he is your first guide. He will often meet your own expectations of what a guide looks like. Many people see a religious figure in keeping with their own faith. Often monks and nuns make an appearance.

There are several criteria guides must meet. They need to:

- Be acceptable to you.
- Meet your expectations.
- Make the greatest impact on you.
- Be appropriate to your level of awareness.
- Arouse a feeling of love.
- Cover your field of interest.
- Help you to find your own answers.

CONNECT WITH THE ANGELIC REALM

One of the most uplifting channelling experiences is when you connect with the Angelic Realm. There is no doubting the validity of this meeting. Inside yourself you will feel enormous love surrounding you. You may feel emotional and have tears running down your cheeks. There can be bright light that not only you will feel, but that others can see around you.

There is a vast host of angels, ranging from the highest such as Metatron and the Archangels down to those of the Angelic Realm who may or may not have taken physical form at some time in their progression. There is no reason why any one of these might not come and speak through you. Often an angel will come as a colour and a vibration without showing himself. By his words you will know the quality of his information.

You may have a preference for one particular angel, and attribute that identity to the presence that comes to you. It is your soul that strives for the connection with the Angelic Realm. It is the quality and understanding of your soul that

ensures you have the most suitable and comfortable contact with an angel.

It may well be your own guardian angel who makes that decision. You all have one angel who watches over you. Allowing him to speak will always be for your benefit since it is his role to ensure you are safe. Your guardian will never lead you astray and will always speak the truth.

CONNECT WITH EXTRA-TERRESTRIAL INTELLIGENCE

We are one. This means that we are all part of the Creation, the Divine Source, the God Consciousness. This includes all the cosmos with its planetary systems. Souls have also incarnated on many planets and have a spiritual progression, as do we. Therefore it is not surprising if a being that is not of our Earth contacts us through you as a channel.

It is recognized that extra-terrestrial intelligence usually has a wider view of happenings concerning our planet and is concerned that we understand our role for its survival. These Space Guides have been around for a very long time. Evidence of their contact can be found in the Scriptures. If they intended harm to us, then they have had lots of opportunity to do so before now. Therefore we can conclude that they wish to help us. If you can maintain a channelled connection with them it can only be to the advantage of yourself and the planet.

Some spirit guides from other planets have had previous incarnations on planet Earth and have a special interest in our progression.

MAKE PREDICTIONS ABOUT THE FUTURE OF THE WORLD

Predictions are given by spirit guides so that we take notice. Predictions are based on known facts prevailing at the time they are made. Conditions are subject to change according to our own actions and thinking. Therefore we control our own future. Spirit communicators are always telling us that we make our own future world. Are we listening?

Some of the predictions made have already come about. However, if they have not, we can change what we do not like and encourage whatever will give us the world we would like to live in.

good. Trust that your intuition is accurate, especially if it what it tells you feels right. We often say: 'It is too good to be true.' Does it really have to be bad to be true? Your answers will always be right if you go with the feel-good factor.

GROW SPIRITUALLY

We all know when something is right and when it is wrong in our actions and words. We also know when what we listen to is right or wrong. When channelling, you will accept words and feelings if they feel good to you. You can equally deny and refuse to accept when the opposite is true. It is your responsibility to know the difference.

You attract to you a spirit in keeping with your own spiritual aspirations. He will present opportunities for growth through his teachings. What he tells you is intended to inspire you to live life according to spiritual values. With his help many of life's challenges will be seen in a more helpful perspective, enabling them to be overcome.

Predictions are worth having, but are often left open to false interpretation. How many are still trying to interpret the predictions of Nostradamus! Go with your instinct when you interpret the messages you receive through channelling. When asking for answers, know that your own expectations and beliefs influence the response. Therefore it is of benefit to you if your expectations and ideals are for the highest good.

Remember that you are channelling through your subconscious soul mind, which will only work for your highest

MEDITATION FOR CHANNELLING

Being able to meditate is essential if you wish to be a conscious channel. Meditation is the first step towards connecting with your soul, guides and Higher Forces for good. There are many types of meditation, all of which are beneficial.

Some reasons for meditation are very similar to those concerning channelling, as listed below:

• To contact your guides and spirit teachers
• To make contact with your Higher Self, your soul
• To take the first step towards clairvoyance and mediumship
• To assist in healing yourself and others
• To enable travel to the past or future
• As the first step towards channelling
• To raise your vibrations.

The method you will need is an interactive one. Those who think that you must empty or still the mind have a pleasant surprise coming.

The objective is to bring back to full consciousness any information and enlightenment that is useful to you. Your mind is going to be more active and more focused in this kind of meditation than in your daily round. Most of your day is spent on autopilot. How often have you driven your car and arrived at your destination without remembering how you got there? In this type of meditation your mind is going to be so busy paying attention to the journey that it will not want or have time to go off in other directions. It will not worry about the kids, the next meal, the office, or anything else. Make this your objective: mind alert, body asleep.

It is easier to channel than to go into deep meditation. Deep meditation means stilling the mind and waiting to see what happens. Active meditation means that your mind will be interacting and participating in the scenes and thoughts that arrive. It helps to decide beforehand your purpose for the meditation so that you can interpret the thoughts and events

CLAIRSENTIENCE, CLAIRVOYANCE AND CLAIRAUDIENCE

When psychic ability is active it may present itself in many ways:

- You may be an intuitive psychic. You sense and feel things rather than see or hear them. Somehow, you just know in your head what has been said or is to be seen. You have impressions of the presence of spirits or feel them in your body. A person of this kind is called sensitive or clairsentient.

- You may have a visual ability. This means you can see in your mind a picture or person. You may think you see with your eyes, but it is the soul that sees and presents the picture. This kind of knowing is called clairvoyance.

- You may able to hear audibly, either as a voice from inside through the soul's hearing, or exterior to and independent of the body. Doing so is called clairaudience. There are variations to what you can do with clauraudient ability. It is useful for relaying messages to others in public demonstrations or private readings.

Psychic experiences such as these during meditation provide personal insight and help put you in touch with meditation guides and with your own soul.

accordingly. Think of it as having a conversation with an unseen person or situation. In most conversations there are questions and comments between those present. The questions and requests you have in you when you enter active meditation will provoke a response either from your own soul or from the spirit communicator. This may come in the form of more thoughts or as seeing, sensing or hearing. This depends on where your psychic ability is strongest in you.

The differences between meditation and channelling

The principal difference between meditation and channelling is not the level of trance, but the reason for engaging in these activities. Meditation is most often used for your personal interests and spiritual growth. What you may learn about your journey and how you may deal with life challenges are assisted greatly through spirit contact during meditation. It is more likely that you will attract your own personal guide, though depending on your reasons for meditation it is also possible to have contact with a Higher Being.

The motives for vocal channelling vary, but generally are not just for yourself but for others who come to listen. The desire to know covers a wider field and often includes philosophy, predictions and teachings of a spiritual nature. Having others present who focus on you as the channeller adds the energy required for a more advanced level of contact. Due to your spiritual motives you will draw to you spirits of a responsible nature, such as the Angelic Realm and the Masters.

Unless you are a deep-trance medium you will retain control in both meditation and channelling. In meditation you will experience contact in the way that suits you best – clairvoyance, clairsentience or clairaudience. You will need to be able to relax your body, whether meditating or channelling. This is so that only your mind is operating and attention is not drawn away from it.

You can experience clairvoyance, clairsentience or clairaudience, either singly or all together, if you are lucky, during a channelling session. Initially you will need to be able to describe aloud how and what you are experiencing. This enables the voice box to be activated so that the spirit who wishes to communicate can step in and make use of an already functioning organ within you.

To do this takes practice on the part of the channeller, as the tendency is to relate events *after* they have happened. The trick is to speak as it happens. The mind must still be keen, questioning and experiencing as you speak. It is similar to having two minds in one head, both communicating,

but with one voice box being used for both intelligences. This takes an intense focus of the mind.

It is helpful if you practise interactive meditation until you are having clear connections. These do not have to be with a guide or spirit being and may simply be experiences. Once you are happy with this, begin saying what is happening aloud into a tape recorder until you are comfortable with the procedure.

Relaxation

There are several points to take into account before relaxing into meditation:

- Do not try to meditate or channel too late in the day. Your body is already programmed and conditioned to sleep at the end of the day and you may drop off instead of entering a meditative state.

- Switch off any phones and ensure that you will not be disturbed for at least 15 minutes.

- Before you begin, say a prayer. This is your safeguard whilst you are in an open receptive state. Your own prayer could be something like this, though it can be modified frequently according to the purpose for the sitting.

Dear Father, I come to you in love. I ask for your help with the work I have pledged to do. [Insert any personal requests.] May there be no invading negative influences, whether it be from within me or without. May the White Light of the Divine surround me. I invite all those guides, teachers, angels or any who wish to come to communicate with me for the betterment of all. Amen.

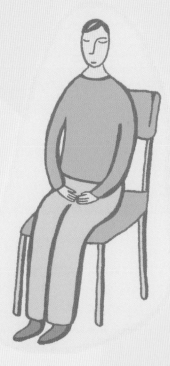

GOING INTO RELAXATION

1 Close your eyes. Feel your feet on the floor anchoring you, keeping you safe.

2 Feel the tension ease out of your limbs. Starting with the legs, allow the muscles to relax and the flesh to become loose. Mentally check that there is no tension in your thighs. Consciously relax the muscles.

3 Go up the body and feel the heaviness of your arms and hands on your lap. Loosen any tension.

4 Breathe gently and become aware of your breathing.

5 Allow your shoulders to sag down with gravity.

6 Feel the energy increase around your throat. Allow your jaw to hang loose with your teeth slightly apart. Feel your cheeks sagging.

7 Your eyelids are heavy. Feel as if you are just dropping off to sleep. You do not even want to open your eyes.

8 Relax the forehead. Ease away frowns or tension. Loosen the scalp.

9 Double check your whole body to ensure it is relaxed, heavy and loose. Simply notice and allow gentle breathing as you drift off into a deep place. Your body is asleep, but your mind is alert.

10 When you decide that it is time to finish, deliberately bring the energy levels down by telling yourself to do so. Consciously feel the weight of your body on the chair, feel the weight of your arms on your lap. Wriggle your fingers and toes. This brings your mind back to physical reality.

Occasionally after a meditation session has ended, you will find it difficult to come back to a 'normal feet-on-the-ground' vibration. You may feel floaty or spaced out. It is easy to deal with this. Eating a piece of chocolate or biscuit is very good for grounding you.

Contacting your own soul
or soul guide

Where is your mind? Where is your heart?
Why are you pulling yourself apart?
There is another part of you
that takes a different view.
If only we could work together
all life's storms you would weather.
Call on me within your being
so I can help you be all-seeing.
I am your Soul Self straight and true.
I pledge myself to work for you,
to place your feet upon the path.
Together we will reach God's hearth.

The words quoted above are a direct message I have received from my Masters and guides. From time to time, I will include these messages when they are relevant to a point in this book. Here they remind you that by allowing yourself to go into a deeper level of consciousness you come closer to your inner being, your soul, the real you that has travelled through journeys in previous incarnations. Your soul is having an experience of living through you in the identity of this lifetime.

When you go into a deeper state your physicality, your cellular body, vibrates at a higher rate. This brings you closer to the vibration of your soul or your soul guide as non-physical beings. Generally we do not see with our physical eyes spirit form, loved ones who have passed over, or ghosts. This is because they vibrate at a much higher rate than us. Imagine you are spinning a bicycle wheel. If you spin it fast enough you will no longer see the spokes, even though they are there. When you raise your rate of vibration and your soul guide or guides lower their vibrations, you become closer to each other and so can communicate more easily.

Your soul consciousness will act as a doorway for these Higher Spiritual Beings and is often referred to as the doorkeeper or guardian angel. Be serious about your intentions. Make time for channelling. Find the slot in your day when it is convenient. If you have a set time or routine when you sit to make contact, not only will your subconscious mind be prepared and waiting, but your guides will be too. Following a set procedure is important for several reasons. Through establishing a routine your subconscious is being programmed to be ready for meditation at a specific time, in much the

same way as your body is conditioned to eat at a certain time, to clean your teeth after meals, to fall asleep when it gets dark, to wake up when it is light.

If you are serious about making contact, but do not have time during the day, then I suggest that the best time for this is between three and five in the morning. I can sense your horror at this idea. Think about it. The airwaves are clear. It is unlikely that the phone will ring; the children will not interrupt, unless you have a young baby. It is unlikely anyone will knock on your door, and you will be able to return to bed and go to sleep easily afterwards.

An evening session is best before and not after the evening meal, especially for those who wish to watch TV or go out. If you feel you are sacrificing your pleasures you might feel resentful or find excuses.

MEDITATION TO CONTACT YOUR SOUL GUIDE

First, remember to turn off the phone and get comfortable. Go through the relaxation process you have learned and be sure to say your prayer to reassure you that all will be well and to bring an increase of energy to flow through you.

1   Remembering that these are mind experiences, feel or see yourself standing at the top of a flight of stairs. Feel the ground beneath your toes. Mentally wriggle them to sense what you are standing on.

2   Accept immediately what comes into your mind. Do not think about it beforehand. Be as sensory as you can. There is a rail to one side. Pretend it is there if you can't see it. Put your hand out to touch it. Is it a banister, rope or something else?

3   Look at the stairs. Are they steep or shallow? Are they wide or narrow? Can you see the bottom? These stairs will take you into the space where your soul resides or where guides wait for you.

4   It is time to do down. Use all your inner senses. Three steps to go: one – two – three. You are at the bottom now. Look around. Take a few steps forward until you turn to the left. Note the type of passage. Soon you will come to a door on the right. This is your door. What is it made of? Touch it, feel it.

5   It is time to open the door and step inside. This is your space. Step in and look around. Note your surroundings. Whatever you see, go towards it, even if it is a drop of water on the wall. Interact with it. You might see a table. Go towards it. There might be a book or a small chest there. Open it. You might see a glimmer of light ahead. Go towards it. If you see nothing, then ask to be shown what you need to see.

6   Most of your input will come in the form of ideas, thoughts, impressions and images. Ask to be told what you need to know. Ask, ask, ask. Question constantly. Make your requests thoughtfully and courteously. You might not see your soul or receive a guide at first, but he will be there. Keep asking. If you don't understand what comes to you, say so. Try not to edit what comes to your mind.

7   You might see an animal. Note how you feel towards the animal. An animal is often presented for you to follow.

It is frequently the guide himself. Your mind will use soul memory to assist you. Trust whatever comes to show the way.

8 When you see a spirit form it could well be your soul guide. Talk to it in your mind and ask to be shown more. You can use such words as: 'Tell me what I need to know' or 'Show me what I need to see'. This is giving your soul guide permission to work with you, which it needs.

9 When your experience feels as if it has come to a natural ending, use the techniques you have learned to close down and return to everyday reality.

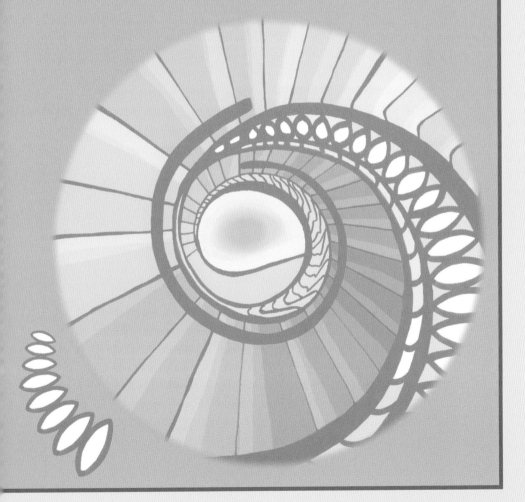

Imagination and interpretation

Imagination is one of the best gifts you can have. We are all products of being imaged. Remember, God created man in His image. You might say you are a product of imagination. What you can image you can bring into reality. First will come the thought or idea. Then the thought takes form in your mind. This can be a deliberate act or may simply arise spontaneously. *Everything* is a sign. Your subconscious tells you what you should notice.

Imagination is essential. It will draw from your memory knowledge of the senses of touch, sight, smell and feelings. If you find it difficult to image, pretend to see something and you will, if only as a thought. Somewhere along the journey events will just happen which you will not have invented, pretended or thought of beforehand. Accept everything that comes into the mind if it feels right and comfortable. Imagination may come as a

thought, idea or picture memory brought forward by your subconscious. Your soul mind will use memories and experiences to put forward an idea or a teaching. Your guide will not use anything that you would reject as being too alien to your mind. Try not to say: 'It is only my imagination' or 'I know this already' and to feel it is not of benefit.

If you go into meditation to reach a goal, use your powers of visualization to achieve it. Allow your imagination to picture the process that will bring the desired outcome. Reinforce the imagery with mind pictures. What you are then doing is creating your own reality.

Do not take everything literally. For example, if in your imagination you are driving a car without lights at night and discover there are no brakes, this does not mean your actual car needs attention. A car

represents a vehicle. You are a vehicle for your soul. You might ask yourself if you are going headlong into a situation without seeing clearly. Alternatively, you might see a ship in trouble on stormy seas. Into your mind comes a thought of a friend who is all at sea and in trouble as a result. So you ask the question: 'What do I do about this?' Another thought will pop into your mind as a response. Accept this as guidance from your soul guide.

Remember that pictures given to you are perceived in your mind's eye, not your physical eyes. What you see is more of a 'knowing' what the picture is, rather than seeing visually. For example, if you take your mind back to a favourite location or memory, you can see and relive it in your head. A lot of people say they cannot visualize. If I asked you to think of a bicycle in your mind, I am sure you could

conjure up an image of a bicycle. Try a scene of the sea lapping on the shore and the rattle of the pebbles as the waves pull back. Can you hear it? What a guide or your soul does is to put a scene in your head, which gives the message he wants to convey.

INTERPRETING A MESSAGE RECEIVED IN MEDITATION

Suppose in your meditation you see a mental image of a lion with a rope tied round its middle. You look harder and see that the rope is knotted and leads up a cliff face. Looking up, you see that there is a ram with its foot on the rope, holding it firm. Your mind is working overtime, and so you ask what the scene is telling you. Because you have asked, a thought comes to you. You realize that someone you know well is a Leo. This man is to hold you secure while you go up in the world. The ram represents someone who will keep you safe as you climb. So, the message is: you have security above and below.

WORKING WITH A SCENE

Here are some hints you can use to work with a scene that your guide provides while you are meditating:

- Ask for the meaning of whatever arrives in your mind's eye or thoughts. Push for more information, if the meaning does not come clearly. Keep asking. You are not only asking your soul guide or spirit communicators, you are asking your deep unconscious, which knows everything.
- Get your spirit self into the scene and go along with it, rather as you would in a lucid dream. In dreams you work out what the meaning is when you wake up, if you remember. The advantage of meditation is that you may interpret and work with what is happening while still mentally active and present.
- Realize that your subconscious gives you what you need to notice. Therefore everything has a meaning. Trust your knowing and do not rely on logic.
- Remember that what you are given is not to be taken literally.
- Try the thought association technique. Whatever thought you are having now,

allow another thought to follow without applying logic. Write down the thoughts as they arrive. Later, read what you have written and try to make sense of it.

You might have a breakthrough about the meaning of a scene while you are doing something quite different. You may see something that triggers a memory that explains all. Or suddenly you find a book or see a television programme that gives you that 'Eureka!' instant when all is suddenly clear. You could also have a dream that explains it all. Or somebody may say something that is meaningful and gives you that 'now I know' feeling. The feeling is like struggling to remember a name that suddenly just pops into your head.

Symbolic meanings, signs and scenarios

The symbols and scenes that come to you in meditation will generally be in line with your own knowledge and interests. For example, if you have a strong interest in Egyptology, you may see a large eye in your meditation – the Eye of Horus, as seen in paintings and carvings on temple walls in Egypt. You may understand that going through the eye will be an initiation process. Later, when you reflect on this image, you realize that it suggests that you are about to begin something new, which requires a certain amount of courage.

However, not all images that you receive will be easy to understand. There may be no continuity in the images, and the meaning of the communication may be hidden in a series of piecemeal and disjointed scenes. Your task is to put the pieces together. Think of it as a game of charades in which each part of a word must be acted before you get the whole picture.

Work on the images you receive as if you are solving a puzzle:

• A car may represent you as the vehicle.
• A policeman may represent an authority figure.
• A baby is a new beginning.
• An owl represents wisdom.
• A pool of water may be the deep unconscious.
• Mirrors are intended to be looked into. Look into the mirror in your meditation to discover the next part of the message.

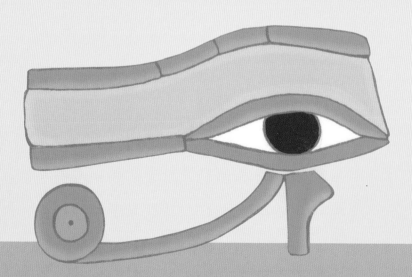

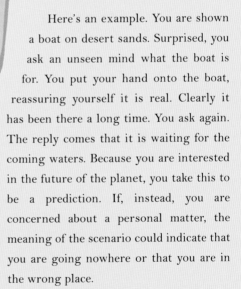

- A ladder going skywards is a clear indication you are to go up in your world, according to particular circumstances in your life.
- If you are familiar with Tarot, you may see its figures, as these will have immediate meaning to you.

Intuiting the meanings of messages becomes as easy as reading a book. Ask for the meaning if you are unclear. You will soon build up a language from the symbolic pictures you receive. Once you have learned this language, your soul guide will use it often.

SCENARIOS

A scenario is a more developed symbolic image. Scenarios often carry important messages because there is usually greater continuity in the story. You may be either an observer or a participant. In most scenarios, you have the opportunity to take your spirit body and mind into the action by having a conversation with a seen or unseen spirit.

Here's an example. You are shown a boat on desert sands. Surprised, you ask an unseen mind what the boat is for. You put your hand onto the boat, reassuring yourself it is real. Clearly it has been there a long time. You ask again. The reply comes that it is waiting for the coming waters. Because you are interested in the future of the planet, you take this to be a prediction. If, instead, you are concerned about a personal matter, the meaning of the scenario could indicate that you are going nowhere or that you are in the wrong place.

Not all scenarios are beautiful and peaceful. Some might contain unpleasant or uncomfortable images. Here's an example. You descend a ladder into a sewer. Dressed in brown overalls, you

UNDERSTANDING RECEIVED SYMBOLS AND SIGNS

When signs or symbols come to you in meditation or dreams, set aside a few minutes to seek understanding of what you have received. Otherwise, you may forget and miss something important. Trust that every sign or symbol carries a message and that your guides will help you understand.

Here are some helpful suggestions:

• Hold the sign or symbol in your mind. Focus on understanding it and trust that a procession of thoughts will come. At any moment a big YES of understanding may arise. Relate this understanding to the thought that preceded it. Go with the YES feeling and do not rationalize. Logic plays no part in the process.

• Get into the habit of mentally asking questions. Your subconscious listens and will seek to provide you with answers to a symbol or sign, if you hold that desire to know.

• Build up a personal language of symbols and signs. For example, if you see a labyrinth it could mean that you will take a circuitous route to get to the centre of things, but there is always a way back or out. How you decide on the meaning will depend on circumstances in your life, your own knowledge and your first instinct, which is always correct.

arrive in an engine room. You are told that the city above is oblivious to the workings beneath its feet. This machinery has to be maintained for smooth running of the city and you are told to grease the wheels. Later, you know instinctively this scenario is about your body, which you have been neglecting.

- Make a list of signs and symbols and add a column of possible meanings alongside. There are many items you can list and thereby have an instant range of meanings ready to hand when required. You can easily build a whole list that your subconscious will use. Your subconscious will choose the correct meaning. For instance, an eagle may indicate soaring close to the Divine source, a legal eagle – the law, or Native American connections.
- Keep in mind that idiomatic expressions may be presented visually. Messages and signs are rarely literal. A fish flopping around may be 'a fish out of water' – someone or something in an unsuitable position. A 'snake in the grass' may signal that someone cannot be trusted.
- The meaning of a symbol often depends on why you asked for it. Keep this reason in mind when you are trying to interpret it. Symbols may mean something entirely different when they apply to your life and concerns than when they apply to another's.

Here's an example for you: within a meditation you may see your own car vandalized with all its wheels removed. It is standing on bricks. After the first shock, you remember that a car symbolizes a vehicle for your soul. No wheels mean it cannot move. Depending on your reason for meditation, the message may be that you can't run away from a situation in life. It does not mean you have to buy a security alarm for your car!

How will you know when you have understood a symbol or sign? As you progress and understanding becomes a habit, your body sometimes gives a physical signal when you have correctly received. You may feel a shiver all over. Some people get a tingle in the head. Others go cold or hot all over. You will learn to recognize the signal that relates to you.

CHANNELLING FOR GUIDANCE AND HEALING

Channelling can be used to seek guidance for your life as well as to bring through gifts of healing from a Divine Source. To channel for a specific purpose, it is important to be clear from the beginning what you are seeking.

Before you begin, give some thought to what you hope to discover. Be specific, narrow the question, and reflect on the type of guidance you wish to receive. Doing so makes your soul consciousness aware of your needs and, through that doorway, the appropriate guidance will present itself.

If you are seeking guidance on an issue in your personal life, clarify the specifics by writing them down or speaking them aloud to yourself. Are you wondering what you should do next for your soul's growth? Is your objective to understand better your relationship with the universe? Are you attempting to connect with a philosopher to gain wisdom or just to see what general guidance may come? Or is there a specific problem that you are seeking to overcome or resolve? Ensure that your purpose and values are in line with each other.

Some seek guidance on whether to take this or that job, to move house or not, to marry this or that person, and on many other issues that arise during our lifetime. Your guide will never tell you what to do, or make decisions for you. He will do what he is trained to do, guide and lead you to reach your own decisions. Channelling often feels like a counselling session.

Maybe, as so often is the case, you do not know what it is you wish to know.

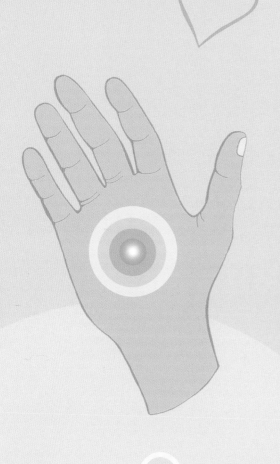

There is a feeling that there is much more to learn and you would do anything to learn it, if only you knew what it was! If this is true for you, acknowledge it and prepare yourself to receive something that is unanticipated.

CHANNELLING FOR HEALING

Often the specific reason for channelling is to seek healing, whether it is emotional, psychological or physical. Perhaps you are personally in need of healing aid, or are seeking healing for a loved one, an animal or pet, or for humanity in general. The spirit world is very happy to be able to assist when the call goes out. By calling on them for help you have already started the process in motion. You can channel healing energies either with the person or animal present or when they are not. In the latter case they may be across the world, since distance is no barrier to healing energies.

What is important is your desire to heal. Call on the Divine Source and use whatever words feel right for you. This Source will send whatever helper is required. Often there is a team of doctors standing by ready to do their work. Go into your higher state of vibration and ask for healing to take place, if it is for the highest good of the individual.

Do not be downhearted if healing is not always effective, for there are times when the person on a soul level has chosen to have pain. Sometimes, if you ask, the healing spirit will tell you why the ailment is present and what should be done about it. It is often wrong to take away pain until a doctor has been seen. Pain might be masking a serious condition and is the body's warning alert. Once the patient has seen a doctor, then you may proceed to continue with the healing, to both alleviate the pain and effect a healing.

Automatic and inspirational writing

A good way to get started on channelling advice for your life is through writing and there are two methods by which you can achieve this: automatic writing and inspirational writing.

AUTOMATIC WRITING

In automatic writing, in which you enter an altered trance state, your hand moves independently of your will. The pen appears to have a mind of its own, because it is the spirit that acts on the hand. The writing goes on without interruption as a continuous flow. It continues until the spirit has said all that it wishes to say. Sometimes there are no spaces between the words and the message can be difficult to read. You often have no consciousness or control over what you have written.

The quality and value of the message are the indicator of the nature and level of the spirit who is guiding the writing.

Discernment is important in deciding whether or not to take notice of the content. Inferior spirits can use this method of communicating for their own mischievous purposes, as well as those guides of a higher nature who have your real interests at heart.

A variation of unconscious automatic writing is semi-automatic writing, in which you feel the physical impulse given to the hand and have the option of allowing the hand to write or not. The words flow rapidly and allow little time for you to assess the content. However, you can stop the process if you wish.

INSPIRATIONAL WRITING

The second method, inspirational writing, is less difficult, as the writer may or may not be in trance. For this reason, it is sometimes unclear whether the writing is from the writer's own mind or not.

EXERCISE IN AUTOMATIC WRITING

Prepare your materials. You will need to have a clipboard and pencil on your lap or to sit at a table. Take the pencil in your hand and make ready.

1 Say your prayer and declare your intentions. State aloud what kind of spirit help you wish to receive. Focus on your highest ideal and values.

2 Use the technique you have learned to go into a meditation level of trance. Go as deep as you wish, almost to a sleep state. And wait.

3 If you are conscious of the hand moving, allow it to do so.

4 Try not to think about what you are writing. Put your thoughts on something else and let the spirit guide your hand.

However, spirit communicators will often inspire writing in individuals who are already advanced souls who wish to aid others with words. Due to their aspirations to assist, these people are considered to be receptive channels by spirits who also desire to help. The spirit communicator connects with the soul of the writing channel, who then feels an impulse to put pen to paper without knowing why. This feeling can come in any place. It is not necessary for the writer to go into a light trance or meditation. Words flow onto paper, with the mind not thinking about what is written until it ends.

The need to write an inspired message may come at any time. One urging came to me while I was on a small island struggling to get ants out of my clothing. I was certainly not in a meditative state or thinking of spiritual matters! Yet the words that came were astounding in their strength. This strength comes through even when read aloud years later. Here is an example of inspirational writing that I have received:

You ask for inspiration. Let yourself be your inspiration. Be *what you aspire to be. You know full well what this is. You do not need another to tell or show you. Is this not true? Allow thoughts of Goodness to flow through you and from you. You know too what these should be.* Be *the one you would most like to meet.* Be *the one you would not hesitate to learn from.* Be *the one whose example you would like to follow. Do all this and the power of your Goodness will create miracles in your life and in the lives of those you wish to help.*

EXERCISE IN INSPIRED WRITING

At all times carry a notepad and a pen or pencil with you. Inspiration comes unannounced, so it is important to have the means to write when the urge takes you, which could be at any time without warning.

1 The urge or knowing you need to write comes in many ways. You may hear an inner voice simply saying: 'Write'. Even when you do not know what it is you will write, begin to do so.

2 When the urge to write comes, it is important not to think about what you might wish to write. The desire to write may be fleeting and needs to be seized on immediately before it disappears.

3 Allow the hand to write the words as the thought comes. Do not stop to read or consider any part of it until you are sure there is no more to come. If you do, the writing will stop or will be from your own conscious mind. The spirit communication will be incomplete, and you will know this to be so.

4 It is also possible to invoke inspirational writing by focusing on what it is you wish to bring to the world, such as a philosophical teaching or wisdom.

5 Whether your inspirational writing is spontaneous or invoked, your natural spiritual values will surface in what you write. Nothing you write will be against your own ethics, as inspirational writing is drawn from knowledge that is given to your soul.

Healing

You would be amazed how many in the spirit world are willing and able to heal through you. The majority of people are able to channel healing energies, if only they realized it. There are many types of healing needs. There is physical, emotional and psychological healing. And there is more than one way to heal.

The route most people take to feel better is to go to the qualified experts in the medical or psychological fields. When this is not effective or when an individual prefers an alternative route, then a spiritual healer or counsellor is usually approached.

It gives confidence to the patient if the healer is also qualified as a therapist, but this sometimes involves a cost that they cannot afford. Spiritual healing that is channelled through spirit beings or spirit doctors is a natural process.

There are many spirit doctors who wish to continue their work and conduct operations on the physical body. Much of this kind of work is well known and accepted in parts of the world such as Brazil and other areas of South America, as well as in so-called less advanced countries where medical facilities are inadequate. I witnessed psychic surgery in a village called Abadiania some several miles from Brasilia. A man called John of God incorporates spirit doctors who work through him. The patients feel nothing at all while he cuts them with a scalpel.

The belief of the one who is ill is helpful to the healing process, but is not essential. This is proved when healing is effective with those in a coma, or with a child, or an animal, or even when the person to be healed is not physically present. This last-named situation is called absent healing or distant healing.

I have experienced personally the effectiveness of distant healing. Derek, the husband of a friend, was rushed to hospital with a heart attack and placed in an intensive care unit. His wife pleaded for help. Although miles away, I prayed for the healing energies to be directed to Derek and soon saw his body laid out on a bed with all the tubes attached to him. To my amazement, silver dust particles began falling over him. My job was to keep this vision for as long as possible. Eventually it was finished.

Derek, home days later, phoned. He sounded excited. 'I have to tell you. When I was in hospital I saw a stream of silver dust all over me. Just like a shaft of sunlight with dust particles in it, only there were no windows and no place it could have come from. It was magical.' I was thrilled. What wonderful proof that absent healing worked.

The main criteria for allowing this force for healing to work through you is to hold compassion and love for those you wish to help. It is also an added help if the family or person who is ill is aware that absent healing will be sent at a particular time. Then they too can focus and pray for healing energies at the same time and, by so doing, increase the chances of it being effective.

AN EXERCISE IN CHANNELLING HEALING

You must first establish some personal boundaries between you and your patient and also ensure that he or she is happy to be treated. The following points are particularly important:

- Establish that the person wishing to be healed has seen a doctor and is under his care, with any necessary medication.
- Sit down and talk together to help you decide which type of healing is required. Although it will be the spirit doctors or Masters who carry out the healing, you too have a responsibility of care.
- Determine in your own mind whether the cause of an illness is due to negative attitudes or hate, anger or resentment towards another. During the healing process you may be met with distressing reactions to the healing. You need to know how to deal with a possible release of traumatic personal history.

- Use your talk with the person to help you decide what healing process to pray for.
- Try to be non-judgemental. You may find it uncomfortable to have your hands on someone whose illness has made him unpleasant to be around or towards whom you have negative feelings. Perhaps you are feeling resentful that the ill person has not done more to help his own condition. My own guide has pointed out to me that it is easy to love the lovable, but it is the unlovable who

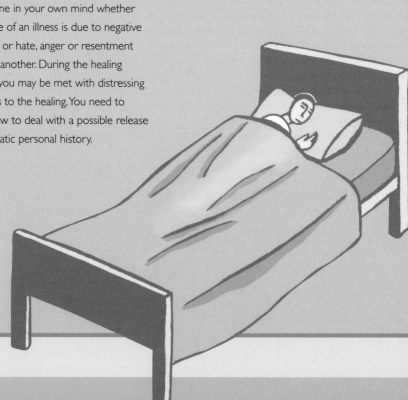

need love the most. Keeping this in mind, it is easier to find compassion within you. Love, not necessarily liking, is a vital component of healing.

- Make the patient comfortable, whether this is on a chair or therapy bed. Place your hands on the shoulders and say your prayer for healing energies. Soon you will feel the flow though your hands from your spirit.

Once you have established all the above to your satisfaction, you should begin the healing process:

1 Say an appropriate prayer before you begin. Who you pray to is your choice. You may pray to your own healing guides or angels, or to the Father or Great Mother or Jesus and let them decide whom to send. Pray for release of the cause of the illness, for pain relief, for full healing or whatever is needed to benefit the patient's Higher Self. Ask for healing energies to flow through your hands; also ask that these energies go to all parts of the body, to each molecule. In this way even those parts that were not obviously giving trouble are covered and improved upon.

2 You will feel energy flowing through you and you may feel a little fuzzy or spaced out. You may be told where to go on the patient's body.

3 You may feel the pain or discomfort in your own body and through this know what to do. You may see by the aura where the difficulty lies and may be directed by this means.

4 No matter how successful you feel the healing to be and no matter how much improved the patient declares himself or herself to be, at no time should you tell him or her to stop medication. It is the doctor's role to make this decision after seeing and assessing improvement in the patient.

5 When you have finished, thank the spirit guides and then stand back and ask to detach your vibrational field from that of the patient.

6 Wash your hands if at all possible.

Guide drawings and psychic art

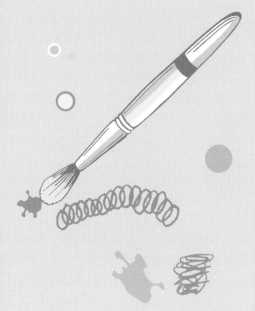

Spirit guides may also communicate with you through art and drawing, even if you have no artistic training. Many excellent psychic artists have never painted before. A guide drawing – an inspired portrait of a spirit guide – might reveal more about the guide's personality than about his physical features. You may not see the person you are drawing; rather, you paint what you feel. Drawing your guide may help to deepen your connection and improve communication.

It is sometimes easier to create psychic art for someone else, as your conscious mind can less easily influence what you draw. For instance, you might draw the face of someone's departed friend or relative. It is also possible to bring through a portrait of a departed pet.

Doodling is another way you can allow your subconscious mind to express itself artistically. A woman I know brings through amazingly detailed and colourful designs while her mind is focused on unrelated things, such as talking on the telephone or watching television. The energy of her drawings is very potent, even when they are photocopied, as their inspiration seems to come from an extra-terrestrial source.

You can try the same technique yourself. Hold a pad of paper and a pencil in your hand while you are watching television, travelling on a bus or waiting for an appointment. Allow the pencil to wander where it is directed. Later, use your drawings or doodles as prompts during a channelling session. Ask your guide for the meaning of the drawings and prepare for the fact that you might be surprised by the answer you receive!

CREATING A GUIDE DRAWING

Lay out your preferred drawing materials, such as paints, coloured pencils or markers and an easel or sketchbook.

1 Use the technique you learned earlier on to enter a meditative state (see pages 22–23).
2 Make your wishes known to the spirit. Ask for a guide to present himself visually. Sit quietly and wait for the mind picture to appear to you.
3 Allow your inner knowing free rein while your hand moves along the paper. Try not to think that the face should look this way or that. Keep your hand ready and allow it to pick up whatever colour or pencil it feels drawn to.
4 The validity of what you have drawn is confirmed when you feel an affinity with the face that comes through or the person you are drawing for recognizes the face. Believe that you can be a psychic artist.

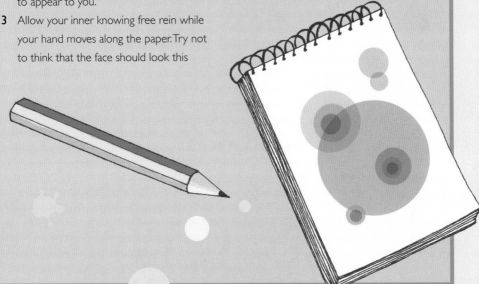

Speaking

Allowing non-physical beings to use your voice is what we generally call channelling. A channel is vocalizing to enable those from the spirit world to communicate using a human voice. It's important, however, that you do not make the mistake of assuming that all spirits who wish to communicate through you are of a high moral level. A spirit able to communicate through you may carry the same morals and personality that he had while in physical life, if he has not advanced since he left. It will be up to you and those who listen to decide if the quality is in tune with your own values.

However, since you will draw to you those most suited to your level of awareness, understanding and values, it is unlikely that you will connect with spirit minds of lesser quality. I tell you this so that you are aware of the possibility. Here are some warning signs to watch out for, which indicate that you may be in contact with a less helpful spirit:

• He uses an overabundance of words without saying very much.
• He uses language that makes you feel uncomfortable.
• He judges or criticizes.
• He speaks over your head.

It is known that among the spirits you invoke there are some who are still incarnated on Earth, but are asleep or dreaming. They may talk to you as spirits and not as men. This does not necessarily mean they are inferior spirits. Remember

that your spirit is the interpreter, in much the same way that a telephone line acts as a means for communication. Your soul will act as a guide or guardian.

A spirit communicator will seek a channeller who is in sympathy with his values and objectives. With accord between both channeller and spirit there is no difficulty in translation. It is helpful to the entity (spirit) if you have at least a basic knowledge of his subjects. It is to your own advantage to learn and gain as much as possible regarding subjects related to your own interests. This way you both advance in progression of the soul and knowledge by working as a team.

You may find it difficult to see yourself as part of a team with a Master Guide or

angel or a well-known personality. If these spirits worked hard in their lifetimes to pass on their knowledge and philosophies, then it is not so hard to understand that they still wish to continue their work wherever they can, and are delighted when they find a suitable co-worker such as you to speak for them.

The range of subjects is vast. You may be interested in philosophy and could well draw to you one such as Plato or Socrates, or a guide who has wisdom to impart. You may have a scientific interest or be concerned for the planet. You may be interested in spiritual behaviour and values. Whatever you wish to come through you from spirit will draw to you a like-minded communicator. This does not preclude the possibility of having a Space Guide using your voice box.

If at any time an entity speaks to you that makes you feel uncomfortable, then tell it to leave. It has to obey. You are in control at all times.

SPEAKING ALOUD A CHANNELLED MESSAGE

Remember that there are several issues that you must address before you make a start:

- Try to establish a regular time for your channelling sessions, maybe once a week or once a fortnight, according to your lifestyle. Whatever you arrange, keep to it, as this is as much a programming of your subconscious to enable clear input as it is programming for the spirit communicators. Whatever you might think, spirits are not just sitting around twiddling their thumbs waiting for you to call. A regular schedule is much appreciated.

- Have a tape recorder handy so that you can listen later and prove to yourself that it is not you who is speaking. If you are channelling alone, have an on/off switch that can be activated with a slight pressure of the thumb. If you have other sitters present, ask one of them to operate the machine when you begin to speak. Bear in mind that there has to be time for relaxing in order to make a connection and it is unlikely to be immediate. If you switch on a tape machine before you are ready and 'in connection' with your guide, you run the risk of the tape ending before anything has happened. This concern would be enough to disturb your mind and prevent contact.

- Treat the spirit communicators with as much consideration as you would a friend or specialist.

Before you begin, remember three things: to clean the room and make sure it feels energetically right for inviting a guest, to light a candle and to say your prayer.

1 Use the technique you have learned to enter a meditative state. Feel where you are as you begin a journey as directed by your inclination or soul guidance. If you are directed to do so, deepen your trance state so that your level of vibration is closer to that of the spirit wishing to communicate with you.

2 Instead of simply experiencing in silence, describe aloud what you are doing or feeling. Also ask your questions aloud. This beginning is merely to get your voice box working so that the spirit communicator can enter more easily. Your mind will be so wrapped up in your journey that it won't get anxious.

3 Don't try too hard. This is one of the blocks to allowing another to use your voice. Relax into the describing process and let it run as far as it wants, while your mind can still focus on the field of interest that has motivated you to try this.

4 Allow your mind and voice to ask questions as they arise and, to your surprise, an answer will come. You will forget it is your voice that is saying it.

5 The transition from speaking to channelling may be so smooth that it will feel as if you are answering your own questions and coming out with information from yourself. It is only when you listen later that it will strike you that the language is not yours and you couldn't possibly have known what you have said. When you listen you may recognize that your voice has changed in some way.

TRANCE CHANNELLING

Trance is a condition between sleeping and waking that allows dissociation from the conscious mind and body, as in hypnosis. It is a state of deep or lighter separation. Trance channelling is when in this state of consciousness a voice or energy is passed from the spirit world through the physical form and voice box of the person in trance. The voice box of the channeller is the conduit for communication and energy, with its soul as the spiritual safeguard for the body it inhabits.

In the deepest trance states, the soul may seem to have left the body. However, it is impossible for the soul to detach from the body completely until death. A deep trance state is more like being in a coma. There is no need to be concerned should you find yourself entering this deep state, because you will not die. A silver cord maintains the connection between body and soul until the end of life.

Sleep is another kind of trance state. During sleep, the soul may journey out of the body, where it may or may not have remembrance of events. This is called astral travelling. Some fortunate people can direct this travel at will.

Psychoactive drugs can induce other kinds of trance states. In the rain forests of Brazil, healers and seekers sometimes use plant substances such as Ayahuasca to induce a trance state. It is also possible to reach a trance state by dancing or drumming, as is done in many indigenous cultures. The Whirling Dervishes of Sufism, which is a mystical form of Islam, reach a trance state by spinning rapidly in a dance ritual.

Hypnosis can also assist one to enter a trance state, during which a hypnotherapist can make suggestions for resolving specific goals. It is not usual for a spirit to speak through you when you are under hypnosis. The information brought forth is generally related to the life experience of the person under hypnosis. However, it is possible for a hypnotized person to bring forward a past life to be assessed. When this happens, a hypnotized person might speak in a different voice and seem to have a different personality, but what's happening is generally past-life regression, and not channelling as such.

Most people have heard of zombies. It is a belief of some West African voodoo

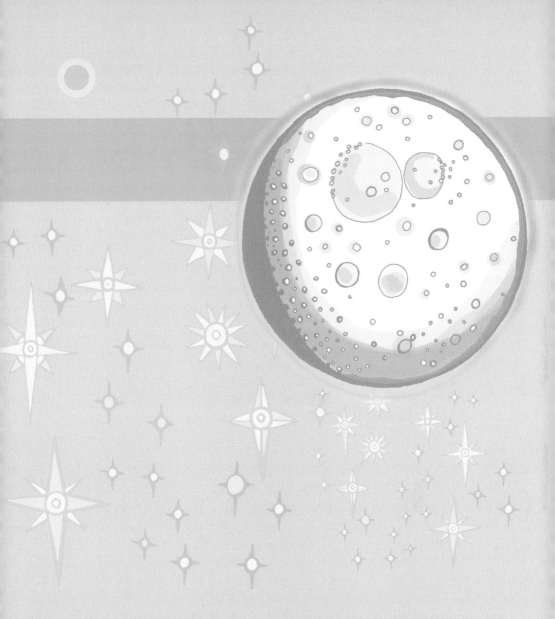

cults and other voodoo cults in Haiti that a dead person is able to be reanimated and function without its soul. This would be another extreme trance state. The truth of this is open to debate and would depend largely on the belief of those concerned.

In several countries of South America and other remote parts of the world, psychic surgeons conduct their work while in a very deep trance. The body of the surgeon appears to function and carry out its duties with ease and he is able to converse normally with those around him. He takes on the personality and skill of the spirit doctor, yet it is clear that his own soul is absent at this time.

Light trance with control

In lighter types of trance, you are conscious of everything around you, such as sounds and movement. In this state, you are able to interject your own thoughts, and voice your own questions or state your opinions. You are in control during this interaction. This state is sometimes known as semi-conscious trance.

When you engage in channelling while in a light trance state, there is usually a mixture of direct information from the spirit entity and the channeller's personality and opinions. Light trance often carries the flavour of the channeller himself.

Many spiritual platform speakers and platform clairvoyants give their talks and addresses in this light trance state, with their eyes wide open and quite able to interact with the audience. You will enjoy light trance and frequently feel as if the information is coming from your own knowing. Much of what you receive will feel familiar to you. This is because the entity speaking will be close to your own

aspirations and will use the knowledge you already have as a base for taking you and listeners a stage further.

In light trance the entity will discuss most questions or subjects that you and others have an interest in, be it personal or general. However, there may be some questions that they may not answer and some subjects they will not cover. One reason is that not all spirit communicators have expertise or knowledge to be able to respond or talk on all subjects. Entities do not know everything, and much of what they give depends on their own level of development and particular interests.

Light trance can be used by psychics when giving readings and bringing through the personalities of those who have died. This is very helpful in that the medium, as he or she is called, can work both with the entity or guide who is assisting and with the spirit of the one who is dead.

Often mediums as channellers are able to amuse an audience by combining their own charismatic character with the messages received from the spirit world. This serves a good purpose because as a result many a person has been intrigued enough to make their own research into the phenomenon and think more deeply about life. It also provides evidence that life continues after death. This belief has a beneficial effect on individuals in dealing with life and its challenges.

Light trance may bring in disoriented or unaware beings, who are likely to come with nonsense or practical jokes. These beings come in order to amuse themselves at your expense. They cannot harm you and you can ask them to leave. This request they have to comply with. Ask for the highest guide to come forward.

When a group focuses together in order to bring through a spirit being, such as when using a Ouija board, it is very possible that one or several present may go into a very light trance state without realizing it. This is when you could attract a low-level spirit with less than high intentions. This is dangerous and would best be left alone.

INDUCING A LIGHT TRANCE

It is very important to create the right atmosphere, so choose a spot for your channelling that is restful and comfortable. Later, when you are more practised, you will be able to go into trance to channel more or less anywhere. You may wish to put on some soothing and spiritual music. However, as you may sit for some considerable time, put the CD or cassette on repeat mode. Otherwise, if it loudly clicks off when it is finished, it could jolt you and end your trance state. Begin with a mental or physical ritual if you feel it helps. A regular ritual conditions the subconscious to prepare for connection. For instance, place crystals in each corner of the room or in front of you. Lastly you might like to set the scene by lighting candles. Candles are preferable to electric lighting as they are less harsh.

It is best if you are calm and in a positive frame of mind before you attempt going into a trance state. If you are in a state of turmoil or distress, wait until you are through this before you attempt to open yourself in order to bring an entity forward to speak through you. Keep in mind that you attract to you a spirit in keeping with your own state of mind. It is also difficult to dissociate from consciousness if you have your mind on other concerns.

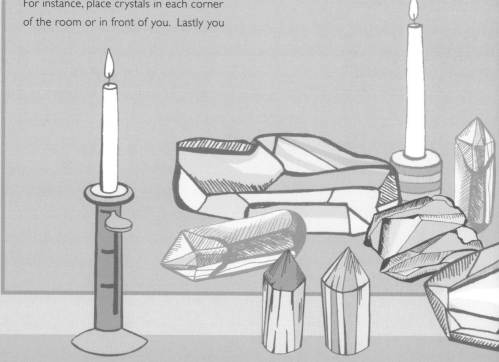

Sit comfortably, and since it is your objective to allow a spirit to talk though you, remain as upright as possible in your chair. This will allow an easy flow of the energies. You will see what I mean if you try speaking clearly when you are scrunched up with your head either lolling back or dropped forward onto your chest.

1   Begin by closing your eyes. It is easier to channel if you keep your eyes closed, though later on you may prefer to have them open. With eyes closed, things or people in the room will not distract you.

2   Ask for the presence of the angels and guides and any who wish to communicate through you for the good of all.

3   Ask for the light of The Divine to fill the room. Energize the room with images of light. You will sense this happening.

4   Visualize yourself immersed in this light. Make your prayer either aloud or mentally, and ask that there be no negative influences around you. The light created will keep out unwanted energies.

5   Spend a few moments relaxing as described in the Meditation section (see pages 22–23). Quiet the mind while imagining yourself floating higher and higher into space. Imagine you are reaching a realm of great spiritual beings and colours.

6   As you immerse yourself in the experience, send out loving feelings for all those you are familiar with and all those who might be having a hard time in life.

7   You will soon realize that your mind is drifting pleasantly. You are in a light trance state and ready to attract to you an advanced spirit who is drawn to you by your thoughts.

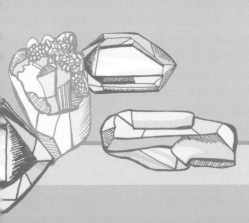

Deep trance

As the term 'deep trance' indicates, this is going even deeper towards a non-conscious state. There are varying levels of how deep one may or may not go. The deeper one enters into a trance state, the more fully removed from the body is the mind of the channeller.

In the deepest state the channeller's soul leaves the body and is taken to other realms by his guides. He enjoys a reality not accessible in a normal conscious state. Usually he has no conscious memory of where he has been. Having said that, there are individuals who do remember and who may relate their experiences later. His guides will ensure his safety and return at the correct time.

Anyone present as a sitter will notice a change in personality and mannerisms of the medium. Facial appearance may change and the tone of voice may differ greatly. In

this degree of trance the entity will speak directly without interference from the personality of the channeller. He may speak in another language, if this is required by a sitter for confirmation or for a private issue. It is worth noting that the spirit acts on the organs of the physical form. These organs do not have the same flexibility for an unknown foreign language. This limits the range of languages that might otherwise have been used.

The entity is likely to be a highly evolved spirit who takes into consideration the needs and level of understanding of those present. He will speak wisely on subjects that are far-ranging and will concentrate on issues that lead to self-growth and development. He will invite sitters to ask questions so that the experience will be similar to having a conversation with a wise and kind person.

It is not unknown with deep trance channelling to converse with an Archangel or one of the bands of angels. Sometimes the evolved spirit takes over the whole body and not simply the mind of the channeller. Those present may recognize a known figure from the past. This change

can be quite dramatic. On occasion a great spiritual leader or one of the recognizable Master figures is seen. The full bodily form or just the face may be evident and described. This may be as a vague suggestion of shape or seen with great clarity. Even though sitters know the medium's eyes are closed, they may see the entity's eyes fully open and looking at them directly while he speaks.

In these instances the sitters feel a great love and compassion coming from the superior spirit and may be emotionally moved. Spirit communication through deep trance channelling is wise without being sombre. These guides bring humour and laughter, but they do not come for entertainment purposes. They like people to enjoy themselves.

You may feel as the channeller that you gain nothing by allowing a spirit to enter and use your body, since there is no recollection while in a deep trance state. However, you will be experiencing at a soul level much that will be of advantage to your soul progression. Your sacrifice of time and energy is always rewarded, even when you are not consciously aware of it.

GOING INTO DEEP TRANCE

More preparation time is needed for deep trance than for light trance. You may feel that the whole day is required. As you go into deep trance more often, over time you will not feel the need to prepare so early. If you wish to channel the highest values from the spirit, keep your mind clear of negative thoughts and reflect on the positive nature of life.

During your day of preparation do not be too mentally occupied with any difficult situations or problems you may have in your life. Go for a walk outside in nature, or along the seashore if you are close enough. It is also best if you do not eat a heavy meal an hour or two before the session. Some do not eat at all that day, but that decision is up to you. If you do eat, make it a light meal.

If you have a job that keeps you occupied during the day, arrange your session over a weekend and have it in the evening. It is not conducive to the energies if you have appointments you have to go to after the channelling. Your restlessness as the time for your appointment and departure draws near will adversely affect the energies.

When deep trance is arranged, it is vital that you have a person who understands the process to manage the evening and any sitters, and operate the recording machine. You as the channeller will have no control over events, or the content and quality of the communication. Your role is to take yourself into a deep state of consciousness and leave the rest up to spirit.

1   Use the technique you have learned to go into a light trance. In this state, you are still able to hear others around you.

2   Stay focused on raising the energy levels and vibrations higher until you forget you have a body. Unlike the interactive meditation technique, you are not required to keep your mind working during your journey.

3   Give yourself plenty of time to relax into a dreamy state. You might like to use the technique from hypnotherapy of counting yourself down. Tell your subconscious to go deeper, deeper, deeper with each breath. Allow your thoughts to arise, but let them pass by and do not dwell on them. You will drift as if you were dozing off to sleep. Soon you will not remember anything at all until you awake.

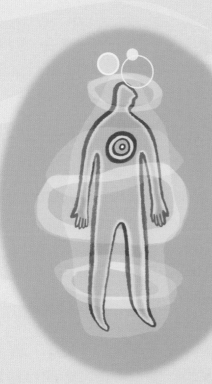

SPECIAL CAUTIONS

- At times you as the channeller may emit a white mist from your body. This is known as the life force or ectoplasm. Should this happen, it is essential that any sitters who are present during the channelling session remain where they are so that the ectoplasm is not broken.

- Should a sitter be affected by the information and possible visual events and become agitated, then your allocated control person must be able to manage the situation to safeguard you.

- The ectoplasm or life force must be allowed to return slowly to the body at the end of the session. This happening is rare these days, but if it occurs it is essential that someone understands and can control things.

Balance and grounding

'You must keep a balance if you want to function on a spirit level.' So say the spirits. They clearly have a sense of humour because at the same time as being told this, I was shown a spirit level of the type used by builders with a bubble of alcohol inside.

A balance is needed. We are incarnated on Earth so that we might experience and learn through a physical reality. If we spent all our time connecting with non-physical beings and trying to be there too often, we would not be carrying out our soul's intention. We need to work, pay our bills and relate to other people.

This does not mean we should forget to behave spiritually. If we keep our thoughts on spiritual values, then we can take them into the work place where they might be needed to uplift those who find life difficult.

Everything is best in moderation. We need feeding on three levels: for our mental body, our physical body and our spiritual body. No one aspect should be sacrificed to the detriment of the others. Equal attention is required for each. This way you will keep a balance in your life. Do not neglect your everyday responsibilities in favour of connecting with spirit. You can do both, of course, as long as one is not forgotten at the expense of the other.

It is important to be grounded after your connections with the spirit world have finished. Eating chocolate or solid food will help. Mentally tell your subconscious mind that you are finished. Give yourself plenty of time to return to normal activity.

REPORTING BACK

- When you feel as if you have gone as high as you can and the energy in your head is as full as you can stand, begin to describe how you are feeling. Describe any sensations or visual images that come to you. You may at first simply have vague impressions of someone around you. You may see colours. It is highly possible you will experience a different feeling in your head or body.

- You may be aware of expansion in your chest or upper body and head. This will be the entity bringing in his spirit body so that you get a sense of his size and form. With this you have insight into his character and feeling of love. You will know instinctively whether the entity is male or female. You may feel facial movements or tickles on the face. Do not be alarmed if he is bigger than you and you feel as if you might explode. It is a sensation only. Not every channeller will have the same experience and you may have only some or all of these things.

- Thoughts and questions will be going through your mind, such as when should I speak, should I start first, when will he speak?

- After you have accustomed yourself to the sensations, it is time for you to speak. Begin by describing your experience, such as how you feel. Express in words your impressions of the culture and identity of the channelled spirit. Describe what you 'see'. Trust your intuition, as it will be correct. It is not necessary to see the entity physically in order to describe it, for it will be a knowing.

- As you continue to speak, either ask a question yourself or have a sitter ask the entity a question. You will feel it is you responding to the question, without realizing there has been a changeover from your voice and thoughts to those of the spirit communicator.

MEETING YOUR GUIDE

The word 'guide' indicates his role, that of guiding. That is his main purpose. He will have chosen to be and will have permission to be a guide for humanity, for a particular person or group. He could instead have had a further incarnation, or gone to a higher dimension for his own advancement, but he chose to sacrifice this for others. In this he deserves our respect.

He may have lived on Earth many times and will have great knowledge of all aspects of our cultures and languages. He is interested in spiritual growth and, through you as the channel, hopes to assist not only those in direct contact, but others who may hear or read his words later.

He will be an evolved and wise soul who uses but one language, the language of thought by which all would be understood. The soul of you as the channeller will be able to translate accurately enough. The spirit guide chooses whom he wishes to use as his instrument. He prefers one who does not consider himself or herself to be superior and will often choose a person who also wishes to help others, regardless of his or her station in life.

It is possible to have a spirit guide who has never incarnated physically as a human being. He will be a highly evolved entity who wishes to be a teacher. It is a pleasure and privilege to be contacted by such a spirit guide.

You may channel the same spirit guide on a regular basis or have a different one each time.

HOW DOES A SPIRIT GUIDE DIFFER FROM A MEDITATION GUIDE?

You generally allow a little longer to go to a higher vibration to reach a channelling guide, longer than you do to work with a meditation guide. You will be more removed from consciousness to allow access for this evolved spirit to work through you.

A guide who comes to you in meditation is not generally concerned with using your

vocal cords in order to be heard. In short, it is not necessary for you or him to speak at all. You may converse with him in your mind only. A meditation guide is there to encourage you personally and help you in your personal quest, rather than for the bigger picture.

It is possible you will have your meditation guide with you for the whole of your life. You will regard him as your guardian, friend and teacher. When you ask a question he will often make suggestions so that you find your own answers. He is more likely to give you scenarios and walk you into the experiences to put over a point or to explain something.

On the other hand, a channelling guide will be concerned with making his views and teachings vocally so that all can be heard and debated later. This guide may use other channellers as well as yourself, should it serve his purpose better. Often a channelling guide is a superior and advanced spirit with much to offer. He tends to be more removed from physical reality than a meditation guide, who is closer in vibrational level to a physically incarnated person.

Types of spirit guides and their expertise

There are probably as many types of guides as there are leaves on trees. Not all spirits are guides, but all guides are spirits. Any spirit that comes to assist or direct can be called a spirit guide.

A spirit guide does not have all the answers or knowledge about all fields of learning. A guide may have expertise on many subjects or just one or two. If you ask a question that a guide cannot answer, the may call on another guide to take his place. Communication occurs most easily between a spirit and a person whose knowledge is well developed in the guide's particular field of interest. If you have knowledge of several subjects, you will likely attract a guide who can speak on a wide range of issues.

It is also possible to communicate with the departed spirits of past experts in a particular field. Deep knowledge of the arts might connect you with Rembrandt or Michelangelo. Philosophy could bring through the spirit of Socrates or Descartes. A fine musician might channel Mozart or Vivaldi. These beings are willing to make contact to encourage deep thinking on matters in keeping with their field.

Some guides will be serious; others, light-hearted and amusing. This variance

does not indicate a guide's level of advancement, but rather his personality. Guides know what will help you to feel at ease with them and present themselves accordingly.

Guides provide different levels of help. A departed loved one might come to assist once or twice, but you should not regard this person as a guide. Your loved one may simply be concerned and wish to connect with you because of family bonds.

GUIDES' NAMES

Try not to be too focused on your guide having a name. It is rare for a guide to volunteer a name. When asked for a name, a high guide will often reply: 'We speak as one mind', indicating that he is the spokesman for many. There are exceptions, of course. The angel Metatron always announces his presence by saying: 'I am Metatron.'

If asked, a spirit guide may give a name that he has used during one of his incarnations or one that suits your expectations. Guides realize that we humans need to have an identity that we can relate to.

HOW WILL I KNOW WHO IS SPEAKING?

If a guide comes on a regular basis, you will learn to recognize his energy and tone of voice. Some guides use the same words as a greeting each time they come. A new guide may give your mind such a strong sense of his identity that you recognize him immediately. When this happens, you have likely contacted a known figure from the past or a celestial Higher Being.

You will learn to recognize specific signs for various guides. When the Archangel Gabriel appears, an amazing light fills the room. You will soon learn the signals that a particular guide is present and recognize signs that provide evidence of the validity of the communication.

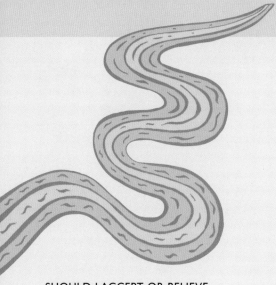

SHOULD I ACCEPT OR BELIEVE WHAT I HEAR?

It is important at all times to use your judgement, in much the same way as you would during a conversation with another person. Much of what is given to you by spirit communicators is to encourage you to think for yourself. You may be stimulated to discover more about the subject so that your knowledge grows by your efforts.

It will be your own decision whether to believe or refute what you hear. Even those who speak to you from spirit will tell you the same. If you ask for more evidence or proof of the validity of the information, they may say they will provide it, if this is possible. They may make a suggestion that will lead you to further research so that you can make an informed judgement.

Your guideline is whether what is given feels right to you and tells you something you would be happy to accept. If what is said makes you feel uncomfortable or is unpalatable, then refute it. It is possible to have predictions which you may prefer not to take notice of, but which others present need to hear. Again it is your decision whether or not to allow this through. If a spirit passes judgement on any other being or is unkind in any way, then do not listen to him and ask him to leave. Guides will come with compassion and love when they speak. They will not, however, dictate what you should do.

DO'S AND DON'TS

- Use your intuition to guide you.
- Decide whether what you hear is believable.
- Ask for further information if you feel you need it.
- If you feel uncomfortable, then refute what you hear.
- Never accept anything that is against your moral judgement.

WHAT GUIDES WILL I ATTRACT?

In the early stages of development you will attract to you a personal guide who will take you to the next stage. Who you have will depend on what it is you wish to do in life. He will make suggestions as to your next step, but it will be up to you whether to take that step or not.

As you progress and prove commitment you will draw a more advanced spirit guide. You will never have one you are uncomfortable with, or that makes demands beyond your time or skill.

You will attract one who has similar interests. If it is healing you focus on, then he will be a healing guide. If you are interested in psychic development, he will encourage you in this.

DO I KEEP THE SAME GUIDE?

There are some people who keep the same guide throughout. Apart from your personal guardian, it is unlikely you will have just one guide. There will be many changes as you move forward. Think of it as a school. You have a teacher for a particular subject for a set period of time.

You learn successfully and go to the next class where a new teacher is waiting. As you move up a level you may cover many subjects and have several teachers coming at different times in the same period.

Eventually you graduate and leave school to try out what you have learned. This is when the Angelic Realm and the Masters come in. Your past teachers, the guides, are always available, should you wish to have a refresher course.

HOW TO RECOGNIZE TRUE GUIDES

When you meet your guide how do you actually know he is your true guide? Is he someone who is truly there to help and not lead you astray?

A true guide will never pass judgement on you or another. The guide is there to guide, not to make you feel bad about yourself. He is there to encourage when you do well and to tweak your conscience when you go astray. A true guide will never flatter. Don't be afraid to challenge. Guides like a bit of spirit (excuse the pun), and know it is right for you to test them. He is there to help you decide for yourself on a course of action. He will help you to see where you may have gone wrong, or take you further when you have done the right thing.

USING DISCERNMENT

Do not accept anything that is opposed to your moral or ethical values. There are occasions when a sitter will draw to the channelling session an inferior spirit. This could be due to the sitter's fears, bringing negative vibrations into the room. As a rule your spirit guide will have prevented this. Sometimes, in spite of the filtering, a mischievous spirit enters simply to have fun with you. Your spirit guide may have allowed this to see how you handle it and to teach you to exercise judgement to discern true from false. All you need do is ask the intruder to leave.

It is important to recognize when a spirit guide uses a great many words, but says nothing of value. It may sound as if he is going to lead to something important, but instead he is speaking for the sake of enjoying the ability to do so. This is not a guide you need, except for the practice.

RECOGNIZING GUIDES BY THEIR VIBRATIONS AND BODY SENSATIONS

As you invite your spirit guide to communicate, there will come inside you a feeling of love and familiarity. If you have several guides who come to speak, each will have his trademark or vibration.

When a guide is an authority figure you will recognize this through your body. You will sit erect and be authoritative in your words. Alternatively you may feel very feminine and soft and will speak in a gentle manner. If you have experienced this before and have known the identity you will recognize this contact as being the same spirit.

Any who are in the room when you channel an evolved superior spirit will also feel and acknowledge that presence. You may feel spaced out. If you feel a sense of humour that comes through, when in normal life you are not humorous, you will recognize this quality as belonging to a particular guide you have had previously.

Another way of recognizing the spirit who is with you is through facial transfiguration. You may feel movement of your facial muscles. This muscular contraction can produce an entirely different expression. You may feel larger or smaller as the guide enters. What happens is that the essence or the etheric field of the spirit guide enters your own energy field and the two merge.

CAN OTHERS CHANNEL THE SAME GUIDE?

There will be some guides who will only channel through you. There are also certain guides who will speak through others if they feel they would be helpful to their purposes. Many well-known channellers only ever have one spirit guide who will only use that particular person. One example of this is Maurice Barbanell, the editor of *Psychic News*, who channelled the Native American spirit Silver Birch. Silver Birch stated that he would speak through no other.

Spirit guides are attracted to each other by similar qualities and often form a group mind. The more elevated a guide, the more likely it is that he will be a spokesman for the group. Since we as humans need an identity, a guide may use a name that best relates to qualities that the spirit group holds, and one with which the channeller feels an affinity. However the name is secondary to the information channelled and is given only so that we may recognize and readily accept messages.

A superior spirit will come in response to like thought, and the desire of the

channeller to connect with a Higher Being, and will take the name of a suitably recognizable person. This is acceptable to the spirit world since what is given through channelling will be in keeping with the collective higher mind teachings.

A guide of this kind will be identified by the personality he has adopted. It is understood by them that we have preconceived ideas as to the appearance and qualities of well-known and loved spirit beings, even though they have lived many lives and taken many names.

Since a guide of this quality represents a well-known identity, he is able and likely to use many channellers. A guide of this level will be able to communicate with many people all over the world at the same time and will not restrict himself to one. This is most likely to be a spontaneous connection from the point of view of the channeller. Although there is

no proof of identity other than in the mind's perception, it is the quality of communication and emotions that will ensure acceptance. Frequently others present will confirm that the spirit guide is this or that person through their senses.

If, however, an inferior spirit borrows a known name to present his ideas, it is necessary to use discernment in accepting (or not) what is said. If you have doubts as to the quality of information, then it is perfectly acceptable to question the identity of the spirit.

Do not feel unsettled if you are told a guide you have thought of as yours alone also channels through another. This means he is a superior spirit guide. If we accept that the overall purpose for channelling is to elevate and unite in spiritual progression, then this sharing may be seen as a positive sign.

There may be occasions when someone who has sat in at your channelled sessions likes your guide so much that he or she sends thoughts to him and attaches his personality to the spirit guide he or she channels. It is the quality of the message that is important, not the name applied.

Meeting your guide for the first time

You are most likely to meet your guide for the first time during a meditation. This will be your personal guide, sometimes known as your guardian or doorkeeper. He will come by this method initially so that you can become accustomed to his vibration and personality in preparation for channelling work.

This does not mean that you will not meet other guides as you continue with the spirit connections, or that you will not channel others. The first one who is your own true guide will stay throughout, though frequently he will be in the background watching, observing and safeguarding you.

He may accompany you as you make your journey inwards or he may be waiting for you when you reach your inner space. He will at all times present himself in such a way as to be acceptable to you. This appearance will be exactly as you would wish or expect it to be. However, he may not show his face until many meetings have passed.

When you first see him it will be at a distance and indistinctly. He may show himself simply as a glowing figure or as a colour that has some vague shape to it. The colour may become his signature so that you can recognize him by it.

You may see him in different guises. He will decide which of these is most acceptable to you and will then adopt that guise for a long period. This gradual process is so that you learn to trust and feel safe in his presence. He will draw closer each time until you are able to describe his appearance as well as his personality. You will be able to describe feelings that he arouses in you.

You will also know that in any time of need you will be able to call on him for assistance. You will feel enormous love and compassion coming from him. It is as if he knows everything about you and is aware of all your fears, hopes, despairs and difficult times that you have experienced in your life from the beginning till now. You will realize that although he knows your deepest secrets, there is no judgement, but only compassion and understanding.

There will be no question that you cannot present to him, no matter how personal or foolish it may seem, for you will know that he will always be kind in his response. You will trust him enough to ask him to show you the darkest corners of your mind. He will do this according to his judgement as to what is suitable for you to face at any given time.

You will have conversations with him as if he were physically present, so that by the time you are ready to speak for him he will trust you to interpret accurately what he wishes to say.

When you are ready to channel your first guide, you will already feel so familiar and at one with him that it will be as if it is you who are speaking your own thoughts. You will be perfectly in tune and at one with each other.

CHANNELLING TO MEET YOUR GUIDE

Follow the usual procedure to prepare yourself to channel your guide:

- During the day of the sitting, quiet your mind and create a peaceful time for yourself. If you can, spend some reflective time in natural surroundings. It is wise not to have a heavy meal for an hour or two beforehand.
- Make preparations in the room where you wish to make the connection, such as placing a crystal in each corner and mentally connecting each with a laser beam of light. You may ask for the presence of the angels.
- If you wish, play some quiet and unobtrusive music.
- Light a candle. Sit in a comfortable but erect position.
- Say your prayer and ask that you be protected from negative influences or thoughts.

Once the room is properly arranged, prepare yourself to channel:

1 Take yourself through the relaxation process, checking that there is no tension or tightness in the body.

2 Open up the energy centres as before starting with the feet (see page 23). As you go up the body you will feel the increasing energy throughout until it reaches a point where you cannot go any higher. As this happens you feel a peace come over you.

3 Ask that you increase your vibration to the highest level that is possible for you. Take yourself to your inner place, as in meditation, and experience the surroundings.

4 If you have any difficulties at this point give yourself an image to work with. This may be a door or an opening of some kind. Go through with the positive expectation of meeting your guide.

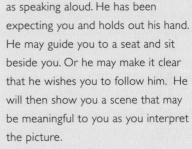

5 Ask that you may meet your guide and recognize him.

6 You may become bathed in light yourself and feel different as you go through the door.

7 See your guide as you expect or wish him to be. You may need to do this as a mind picture if you are not very visual. This is acceptable and as valid as clear seeing. It will feel as if he has been ready and waiting for you.

8 Walk towards him and greet him in your mind. Speak to him in your mind. This kind of communication is as real as speaking aloud. He has been expecting you and holds out his hand. He may guide you to a seat and sit beside you. Or he may make it clear that he wishes you to follow him. He will then show you a scene that may be meaningful to you as you interpret the picture.

9 You can observe his appearance and how he reacts to your questioning mind. This will help you in future meetings. He will know what you are thinking and know how you are reacting inside.

10 Your mind and emotions need to be alive and not passive in this interaction. Your guide will appreciate your participation in this experience. Both his and your energies and minds are required for a successful meeting. He will be assessing how best it would suit you both for future occasions by your reactions to this first meeting. If you are nervous he will proceed with more caution next time.

Enjoy the experience.

What kinds of questions do you ask?

Once you have made contact with your guide, you have the opportunity to ask those questions that have been inside you for so long. If you are asking your meditation guide, or are channelling alone or with just one friend, then you might want to ask about your personal life and any life situations that need clarification. For instance, you might ask:

• What is my soul history?

• Have I lived before?

• How can I resolve the difficult relationship I am having with [some friend or family member]?

• What is my true career?

• How can I achieve my career goals?

Alternatively you may prefer to keep your questions general, but still personal to you. These may be:

• What is my spiritual path?

• How can I achieve spiritual growth?

• What am I here to learn in this lifetime?

• In what way can I use my creative talents to best effect?

• How can I continue to love people when they are unkind to me?

• Why do my family members create such problems? Is this karma?

If your guide is a channelling spirit then your questions will be for the benefit of not only yourself but others who are present. These would then be of a general nature and of interest to all. They may be:

• When does the soul enter the body after conception?
• How does the spirit world view suicides and abortions?
• How does the spirit world view the future of our planet?
• Are we alone in the Universe?
• Will there ever be peace on Earth?

It is helpful to have a tape recorder (operated by a sitter, if possible, otherwise operated by yourself) so that the questions and answers may be debated later on. Sitters may also pose questions of their own. They may have interests that are different to yours, which will bring in a fresh way of looking at the world. They may ask:

• For the name or identity of the spirit guide speaking.
• How to deal with the loss of loved ones.
• What is it like after death in the spirit world?
• Will we ever beat the drug problem?
• How can we change the world for the better?
• Do our souls go elsewhere while we sleep?
• Are we obliged to reincarnate or can we refuse?

You or they may make requests, such as to explain the purpose of religion; to show us how our future world will look; to discuss the subject of karma and its effects; or to tell us about global changes occurring on our planet.

THE RIGHT AND WRONG WAY TO FRAME QUESTIONS

Try not to ask questions all at once and listen to the responses as they come. If the question is too long and complicated, then this will confuse the channeller. Keep it short and concise. Phrase the questions in short stages, a piece at a time. Remember the soul consciousness of the channeller is acting as interpreter for the thought that is being transmitted by the spirit guide. It needs time to process the question to the guide.

In the early days of channelling there is frequently a delay in getting a response. Be patient while the voice box is being prepared. Be open to taking the original question further so that there is eventually a full answer. You may follow a guide's reply with:

• What do you mean by that?
• Please explain further.
• Yes, I understand, but...
• Please show us how this works in practice.

What you are doing in this way is pushing for more information and interacting with the mind of the spirit guide. This is particularly helpful if you receive just yes and no answers that lead nowhere. Often the yes and no responses are due to your nervousness as a channeller or to doubting your abilities, and not to the inability of the guide to answer.

Do not expect the guide to have all the answers to your questions. Some questions may be outside his field of knowledge. Other questions may be outside the field of knowledge within your soul memory. When this happens there may be no response at all or you as the channeller will say: 'I am getting no reply.' The guide may also say that this is not possible for him to answer.

At times there are so many questions waiting to be put to the guide that all speak at once. If you are channelling with sitters in the room, please ask one person to speak at a time and allow the first question to be fully covered and answered before presenting the next one. Allowing a little time between each question will give the channeller a chance to clear the mind of information from the last question.

No question is too simple or too stupid to put to a guide. Often we are afraid to appear foolish or ignorant by asking a basic question. It is usually the case that others are delighted that you have asked what they were too timid to do.

HOW TO ASK YOUR GUIDE A QUESTION

Allow yourself plenty of time to get into a deep state of relaxation. Feel the energy getting greater and greater until you feel you have someone with you. You may still wait a little longer and enjoy the connection if you wish. After a while you will feel the urge to speak. This is when you may begin to welcome him and ask your first question.

When you as the channeller ask a question of your guide, do it verbally and not just in the mind, so that it can be recorded on the tape recorder. It is annoying to hear the reply when you don't know what the question was. You may think you will remember later, but you probably will not. Likewise it is helpful if sitters speak up when they ask a question, so that the voice may be heard on the tape when listened to later.

It is also useful to have your questions prepared before the sitting. This way the wording may be thought out and simplified. You may also like to have other people think of questions in advance and present them to you, or to your sitters, to be read at the appropriate time if they are present at the session. This way you will not have had time beforehand to think about the questions and possible answers.

TIPS FOR ASKING YOUR GUIDE
THE RIGHT KINDS OF QUESTIONS

- First of all decide what kinds of questions you wish to ask. These may be of a strictly personal nature and best for a private sitting. Or you may wish to ask more general questions and have others present. It is important to give some preparation to the questions you will ask.

- If there are several questions, try to have a logical flow to them instead of having them arise haphazardly. The guide will answer more easily than when questions arise by chance. One question may lead to a themed subject for one sitting.

- The tone you take with your guide will depend on how you see him. How you feel about him will also dictate the kind of questions you would be happy to pose. If your guide is someone you would consider to be learned and philosophical, you would probably prefer to put questions on deep matters. If, however, he is your personal long-term guide then the questions posed may be closer to your own spiritual direction and ambitions.

- Thinking seriously beforehand on who and what level of spirit guide you would like to channel will help you decide on the range of suitable questions.

- Try not to ask questions to which you already know the answers. Your guide will know that you already are aware of the answer. Why waste his time when there is so much more to learn? He may well answer with a question of his own, so that you realize you have the answer if you look for it.

- Be aware that a serious spirit connecting with you for your benefit does not appreciate futile questions, but will answer with pleasure any that will encourage you in your personal growth.

- If you ask a question regarding your own precise personal future, your guide may not answer, as it would influence you in how you make your choices and actions. It could make you neglect the present. This he is not allowed to do. If you persist in asking, he may leave. He is allowed to give general guidelines providing you do not ask for specific details. The reason for this is that the future is dependent on

your actions and your thinking, and is not precise or certain.

- You may ask your guide if he is willing to help you understand and progress spiritually. This request is giving him permission to teach you, even when you have not asked a particular question. Your guide will not encourage you to depend on his guidance too much, since this would lead you to lose your own initiative. So often learning comes only through experience. You may ask how you can gain wisdom and he will present you with the means to obtain this. You may ask for courage and he may show you a difficulty that you need to overcome.

- Not all answers come at the time of asking. Try asking what you wish to know in different ways. Think of your questions as a means to gain knowledge and awareness rather than as making decisions for you.

DEEPENING YOUR PRACTICE AND SOLVING PROBLEMS

There will come a point when you will be able to go much deeper into trance and have less influence over information given by the spirit guide. As in all things the part that is exercised the most becomes the strongest. This is true of channelling as well as physical activity. The more you sit and practise meditation and channelling, the better and easier it will be. It is the frequency of sitting that maintains the connection, rather than the length of time spent at each.

When you sit to channel, give yourself much more time to go through the relaxation process. You might feel that nothing is going to happen and that you are wasting your time. At these moments it helps to remember how wonderful it all was when you first made contact. The practice does not become a 'must' or 'should' session, but one that you look forward to.

Give yourself a mental image of going deeper and deeper down the tunnel to your soul. Experience the sensation of this for as long as you can. This will take your mind off worrying about going nowhere. Ask for your guide to be with you and at the same time mentally see your energy field expanding as far as it will go. Focus your memory and visions of your guide, as this will bring him near to you. Soon you will feel a physical shift in your energies and you will know you have connected as your vibrations merge.

DEALING WITH DOUBTS

You would be unique if you didn't have doubts and there will be times when for all manner of reasons it is difficult to make contact. This can happen to the most experienced channellers. If this occurs, give yourself a rest for a short time and do something completely different from channelling. There is nothing wrong with you. Often the atmospheric airways are not clear, which can affect your own transmission in much the same way that magnetic changes in the atmosphere affect television reception.

Doubts come in other ways too. The most common worry is whether the information you channel is from yourself and not from the guide. 'It is only my imagination' is a common cry. When you feel this way, remind yourself that your

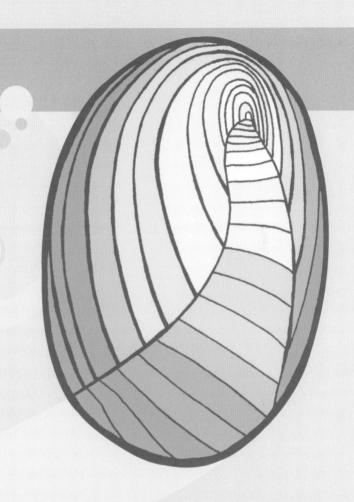

mind and the guide's mind are connected, making you as one. Of course it feels as if it is coming from you.

At times doubting is simply the ego consciousness that wants the control it had before. A part of you wants to go back to the comfort zone of doing nothing. Ask your ego if it would make you happier if you dropped the channelling.

With each contact your knowledge and natural wisdom will grow. Soon you will find that this will come out in your everyday world and you will hear yourself spreading this wisdom. Building a stronger connection with your guide will help you to ask within whenever a problem comes up. The wisdom to deal with it will become quite natural to you.

Raising your vibration

Why would you want to intentionally raise your vibration, and what does that mean exactly? The purpose of increasing your vibration is to bring you closer to those of the Higher Realms, thereby making contact with spirit guides easier.

Your body is composed of atoms, which are never still, but which vibrate constantly. Your vibration is much slower and denser than those in non-physical dimensions. Everything moves much faster in the spirit world, so fast that you cannot see, hear or feel beings there from your physical world unless you first raise your own vibration.

When you learn through meditation to deliberately raise the level of your vibration, and the guides bring theirs down, you are able to meet at some point in between. The guides often help in this process by controlling the pace at which you progress.

The experience of raising your own vibration can be quite physical as your etheric, mental and physical forms try to

maintain equilibrium. You might experience headaches or feel as if your head will explode. You may feel extremely hot and perspire copiously. Or you may feel very cold, even to the point where it takes hours to warm up again after the session. Change your rate in stages and do not force it. If the energy gets too painful, deliberately and consciously bring the energy level down again.

Each time you practise you may experience an energy barrier through which it may seem painful to push. It is worth taking yourself just that bit further, for when you do you can suddenly find yourself clear, with no pressure. The next time you sit you will not meet the same barrier and you will be able to increase the levels just that bit more until you reach the next barrier.

Over time, depending on how often you deliberately try to raise your vibration, there will be no resistance or such tremendous pressure in the head. I suggest you do not try too often and let your instincts tell you when it is time to try again. It takes many sessions to bring your vibrations up so high that others may no longer see you while you channel. It is an enjoyable experience, with no effort at all.

CHANNELLING WITHOUT RECEIVING A MESSAGE

There are many ways and reasons for channelling and not all involve getting a message. When channelling is mentioned it is often thought of as vocalizing for the spirit world. However, the channelling state can also be used for bringing through healing energies. No words are used and no messages given in many cases.

Many books have been channelled with guidance from spirits while keeping a focused mind and simply allowing the words to flow. The spirit world is willing to connect with your mind when you are considered capable of understanding and accepting the ideas they wish to put forward. This is true when you have made an appeal for inspirational guidance, but may have only a vague intuition that a response has come from spirit.

It is possible to channel colours and geometric shapes, which in themselves do not appear to hold a message. Everything received from spirit has an energy that affects the recipient. If it feels good, accept it. It is quite possible for a spirit guide from the highest levels to channel his essence into the room. You and any present will feel this and react accordingly. Archangel Gabriel comes with such a bright light that the room lights up even if

it was previously darkened. No message perhaps, but great joy and peace come with his visit.

You may channel scenes that you are able to describe, but which do not appear to hold a message. They may be given so that you can discover the meaning for yourself. If you channel symbols, you can later research the meaning if you wish to.

Psychic art is another method of channelling for those who are drawn to do it this way. The guide will enable the soul to see with enough detail that the artist can paint an accurate picture.

CHANNELLING MORE FREQUENTLY

How often you sit to channel will depend on how much time you have. This may seem an obvious statement, but is often overlooked. Decide in advance whether you can put aside a regular time in the month or week. Channelling is not to be picked up and put down just as the mood takes you when you have not established a set programme.

There are no fixed rules as to how often or infrequently you should sit. Your connection will be stronger if you keep to a regular schedule, irrespective of how it is arranged. Your spirit guide will already be waiting for you when you have established a regular time for channelling. He will be waiting as the hour approaches and you will feel his presence in the room even before you go into your relaxed state.

If you wish to channel more frequently than you have been there will be no objection from the spirit world. If you are channelling once a month, then more frequently could mean twice a month. More often than that could be each week, and so on. The important thing is to keep to the arrangement. Naturally there will be times when it is impossible to keep to the regular slot. Your guides understand this too. Simply send up a mental message to that effect.

What we have said above relates to serious channelling endeavours. However, in addition to the regular times you may also channel whenever you wish and for the slightest reasons. This might be for a few moments only, when you 'talk' to your guide. You would do this without going into a trance state, perhaps while washing dishes or gardening. In other words, while your mind is not thinking about anything in particular.

The more frequently you connect with your guide, the stronger will be the bond between you. Providing you do not neglect other aspects of your life and keep a balance, all will be well. If your guide feels you are spending too much time with him and not enough with your physical world, he will withdraw for a short time.

RAISING YOUR VIBRATION TO THE HIGHEST

When you sit with the intention of raising your vibration, put aside the desire to go on your usual meditation journey or to meet with your guide in the normal way and receive messages.

There is no need to prepare mentally during the day on which you attempt to raise your vibration. You can instead engage in physical work or activity so that you burn off the energies of the body and feel deliciously tired, but not worn out, by evening. This can be a walk, housework or gardening. Do whatever you enjoy, but which engages the body.

- It is still helpful to have light meals only, and nothing except a drink for an hour or two before you sit.
- Prepare the room as usual in whatever way you have found to suit you when you meditate or channel. This includes lighting one or more candles.
- Invite the angels and guides to be with you. Their presence will add to the energies and raise the vibrations in the room itself. You do not need to be able to see them, for having invited them they will be there. Have you ever walked into a room where spiritual work has been conducted and felt the wonderful energy around you?
- Relax, but make sure you are sitting in an upright position. It is even more important to do this if the energies are to flow easily through you.
- Uncross your arms and legs. Allow your hands to rest, unclenched and open, on your lap.
- Say your prayer and ask to be surrounded by white light.
- State your desire to go to the Highest Vibration. Ask for help from guides to do this. They act as monitors and ensure that you do not go too high too quickly. Think of it being as necessary as when a diver goes to the surface or descends and must do it slowly or be damaged.

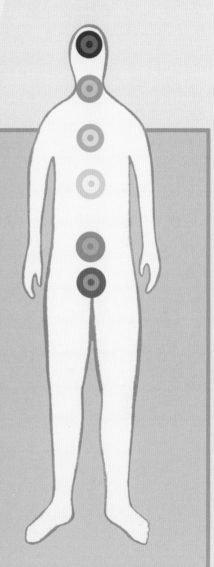

1   Imagine a flow of energy entering the soles of your feet. It might help to see this as a flame that does not burn. Allow this to course up your legs to your base chakra (energy centre), activating it fully. See it flow up your body, opening fully each chakra as it goes up with increasing energy. Ignore the urge to speak.

2   Energy reaches your forehead, which feels as if it will burst as the energy expands it. Focus on increasing the energy until it becomes as much as you can stand.

3   If you have the need for a break, ask your guide to lower the level until you are ready to bring it on again. You may be extremely hot or cold. You may begin to shake.

4   If at any time you wish to stop, know that you can do so. Remember that this process may take many sessions.

5   Feel energy go to the crown of your head. Visualize this opening and see the energy of Higher Beings join with yours.

6   You have achieved the first stage and can now reach higher vibrations without experiencing discomfort.

Problem solving

There are a number of problems that you may well face in the course of your channelling. Do not worry. We are all likely to face them at some time or another. I have listed some of them here and also outlined how to resolve these situations.

WHAT IF YOU CAN'T MAKE A CONNECTION?

No matter how successful you have been in the past, there is bound to come a time when you can't connect with the spirit world. This happens to almost everybody at some time or other. You will wonder what you have done wrong. You will ask yourself if you have displeased the guides in some way, even when you can't imagine how. You may blame yourself for neglecting to meditate more often, and perhaps they have got tired of waiting.

Don't panic! The first thing to remember is that they have not abandoned you. They have not gone anywhere. Time is of no importance to them.

If you have a problem getting in touch with your guide, after previously making contact easily and without any effort, simply go back to how you did it at the beginning. Imagine you are doing this for the first time. Start again as you did when you first learned how to relax, and make your journey down into your inner being in meditation.

Don't skip any part of the process. Take your time. Practise again using your inner senses, such as touch, smell and

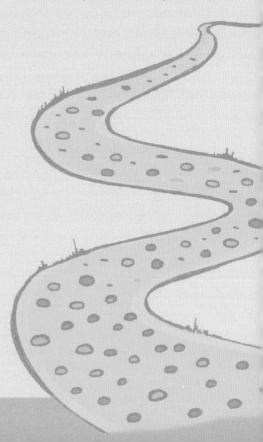

sensing. Go down the stairs of your mind using all your creative and imaginative powers. Have an exciting adventure in your journeying down. This may be exactly what your guides wish you to do. They might be urging you to explore further by yourself rather than relying on them to provide.

Try not to think of connecting with a guide, but see what the journey brings as you go along. The role of a guide is to teach and show the way, but there will come a point when you do not need guidance and are ready to make a journey alone. All you really need is the companionship of your inner being, your soul mind.

A CHANGE OF GUIDE

When there is to be a changeover there can be a problem in connecting with the guide as before. This gap is so that you spend some time assimilating what has been taught previously and must try it out in the field of life. Guides will not give you

more than you can handle and need to leave you to your own devices at times. It is a little like having a vacation after term time. You will have reached the next stage of awareness when a new guide will come to take you to the higher level. He may be there to open up a new way of thinking or to teach a new skill. You will feel a loss of course. However, your first guide will always be around, should you really need him to be with you.

To resolve this dilemma, go back to basics. Continue to sit and meditate even if you have reached the notion that you will not get anywhere. Accept your creative journey as a valuable link, even though you imagine you are not making contact. Each time you sit your innermost thoughts reach their destination. Think about connecting again. Create a guide in your mind. This is connection whether you are conscious of it or not.

WHEN IS CONTACT NOT APPROPRIATE?

The answer is when you are low or angry. All of us have ups and downs. You might think that this is exactly when you need to contact your spirit guide. However, this is not advisable. If you are unwell or upset or angry over something, then this is not the time to open yourself up to spirit. Why?

First of all your energies will be low and not exactly positive. Yes, you may succeed in opening to spirit, but to what level and quality? It is when you are low that your deepest fears can manifest under trance. Not only will this be disturbing, but will attract to you spirits of similar mind. If you are angry over something this will draw to you similar energies. It is more helpful to pray and ask sincerely for wellbeing to return.

BECOMING TOO DEPENDENT

Think of your guide as a parent who has taught, encouraged and been with you as you try out many experiences. When your guide feels that you need to deal with a problem or situation on your own, he may withdraw contact and stand back for a while to see how you get on without him.

This will be true if you have got into the habit of calling him whenever you need. It may be time to 'tap in' to your soul consciousness instead and find your own answers.

GIVING UNINVITED MESSAGES

Some individuals are so good at connecting with their spirit guide that there is a tendency to pass on information whenever and wherever it comes. This is usually of a personal nature and can be for persons known to you or unknown. Unless the message is of vital importance it is not always the time or place to give it and may be regarded as interference by the recipient, however well-meaning you are. If you feel you must pass the message on, feel your way first to test how it will be taken.

RECEIVING UNINVITED CONTACT

Your guide is your friend and, as with all friends, you may not wish to be with them all the time. Your guide does not come uninvited. Because we do not make contact by telephone or letter, but through the mind, we are not always aware that when we think of our friends in spirit we draw them to us. Often these contacts are those we have loved while they were alive and are not necessarily guides.

You may be contacted by spirits unknown to you. These may turn up any time, when you are cooking a meal, out with friends or watching television. This is a form of intrusion.

If you do not want this, it is easy to get them to leave. You simply ask them to go and to come only when invited. A true guide will only appear when you invite him and will not intrude on your privacy at any time. He is not watching you all the time and has other things to do.

HEALING CRISES

Sometimes during healing work, spirit will know when it is not appropriate for a patient to be healed and will not connect. You will not feel the familiar surge of his energy. Accept this.

Dealing with doubts

You would be unique if you never experienced doubts about what you do or receive. As your work with channelling progresses, you may experience doubtful thoughts. As an exercise, take a piece of paper and list any doubts or questions you are having about your channelling. Then answer each as if your guide were speaking through you, offering wise advice and reassurance. Here follows an example of such a dialogue:

WHY AM I HAVING ALL OF THESE DOUBTS?

Doubts help to keep you balanced. Doubts act as circuit breakers when you might be tempted to overdo contact with spirit at the expense of the physical material world in which you must operate.

WHAT IF MY FRIENDS AND FAMILY THINK THAT I'M CRAZY?

Let your friends and family see that you conduct yourself responsibly and they will not think you are strange.

AM I MAKING THIS UP? IS IT MY IMAGINATION?

Don't deny your imagination, especially if you imagine something you would like to have, or someone you would like to be. Don't say: 'Oh, I'm only getting that because I want it.' If it is what you want, so much the better. Go for what you want. It is your Higher Self, your soul, that is providing images and thoughts while you are in a meditative state. It will only give what it feels is right for you.

AM I INTERPRETING CORRECTLY WHAT I RECEIVE?

Change the word 'doubt' into 'discernment'. Think about how you have come to trust your guide. Has he led you astray or have things gone badly wrong for you since you made contact? Or has life been more meaningful as a result of greater understanding? Where has all this help come from if not through interpretation of what he has said? Your discernment on what to accept or discard has brought through only what is beneficial. You may not be interpreting exactly word for word, but clearly enough to be accurate in meaning. In the same way that you trust your guide, trust yourself.

AM I CREATING A PICTURE OF MY GUIDE OR DOES HE REALLY LOOK LIKE THAT?

Your guide will present himself in keeping with your expectations and past life connections. He is able to work with your mind and be whatever will impress you the most and be most pleasing to you. So of course you are creating a picture of your guide, and doing so is just as it should be.

AM I WASTING MY TIME? WHAT USE IS CHANNELLING?

There is no such thing as a waste of time, for all is experience. If you are enjoying the experience and gaining knowledge, then it can never be a waste of time and is useful to you as well as to others. What you gain in understanding will inevitably be passed on, whether you do this by writing or by speech.

CHANNELLING ANGELS, MASTERS AND SAGES

After you have been channelling for some time, and as your spiritual understanding deepens, you are likely to make connection with elevated spirits, such as angels, Masters and sages. These Higher Celestial Beings recognize that your objectives are the same as theirs – to serve humankind. They become your guides in order to act as role models as you try to bring their qualities into your own behaviour and thinking. As you do so, you come closer to them in spirit.

Depending on the status of the entity within the hierarchy of the Celestial Realm, channelling an angel, Master or sage can leave you breathless with awe. You will have no doubt as to the validity of the appearance. The experience may have a lasting effect, and many will comment on the glow that surrounds you for some days after the event.

When you contact a superior being approach him with respect that is his due according to his rank. However Higher Beings do not respond well to flattery or worshipful approach. They will also speak to you in direct simple language. No matter how elevated the spirit who contacts you, the clarity and helpful tone of their messages tells you that this communication is of value and should be accepted.

WHAT OTHER ENTITIES CAN BE CHANNELLED?

All levels of spirit form may be channelled if they wish to be and if a suitable channeller is available and willing. The kinds of figures who appear depend on your understanding and desire to know. Here are some of the different beings you can channel:

Animals

The spirit guide may present an animal that comforts and is of benefit to the channeller. It is the spirit of the guide that has done this and not the animal itself.

Elementals, fairies and beings of legends and myth

Although it is uncommon, channellers may invoke elemental figures, fairies or being from legends. Keep in mind that the value of the message received from such a source is more important than the spirit form that is manifested to transmit the message.

Great historical figures

You may channel such experts as Socrates, scientists or great writers who may wish to continue with their work through you.

Great religious figures

You may bring great figures from ancient religions, such as Poseidon, Abraham, Moses, Thoth or Horus. It is possible for spirits to show themselves as archetypical figures if they feel it will be of assistance to awaken something within you. You may also channel figures from your current religious beliefs, such as Mary, Buddha, Vishnu and others.

Channelling angels

Angels are delighted to be channelled and have allowed this contact throughout the ages. You may channel angels for healing work, for protection and inspiration, or simply to make you happy. Angel connection touches The Divine within you and brings you into a happiness that borders on ecstasy.

Though loving and helpful to people on Earth, angels are not weak in any sense. They have the power to change the Universe if it is considered necessary. Angels protect human beings when their lives are threatened, and are co-workers with human beings in bringing light into the hearts of all. Channelling an angel helps you bring light into the darkness that many are feeling in the world. Through you angels can inspire others to go on to greater things.

THINGS TO BEAR IN MIND WHEN CHANNELLING AN ANGEL

- Angels generally come unannounced. There is a vast order of angels and each has a role to play. An angel with a message for humankind will appear to guide you when the time is right. This is not to say that you cannot ask for a particular angel with whom you have an affinity.

- If you question whether the guide who comes to you is an angel or an inferior spirit masquerading as one, trust your feelings. Channelling an angel is a sublime experience that cannot be confused with channelling a lesser spirit. You will experience a feeling of love, not only for you, but filling the room for others to feel.

- If you have a strong preference for one angel above others and call on him when you are in trouble, it is likely that you have a working connection with him. The Archangel Michael, for example, has many people working for him at all levels. If you are part of Archangel Michael's band, he may present himself with his sword in hand so that you recognize him.

- When an angel is channelled through you he will not be verbose, but will answer your questions briefly.

- You may be wondering why so many angels are making themselves known and contacting human beings these days. Perhaps it is because we have grown enough spiritually to make contact easier. Perhaps it is because our need for the love of the angels is greater than ever. Many Archangels work with us and come when called, if there is a specific and urgent need. Feel blessed if you channel one of these messengers of God.

CHANNELLING A MESSAGE FROM AN ANGEL

The first step in channelling an angel is to decide who it is you wish to come. Here are some of Archangels and their qualities to help you decide. However, it is not necessary to know the names of all the angels. When you have decided what it is you wish the communication to be about, the appropriate angel will appear. He may not give you a name unless you ask.

It is important to decide beforehand what you wish to know or have help with. Nothing is too banal or too complicated. Prepare yourself and the room as usual. It is possible to purchase 'angel essences' that help you connect with particular angelic vibrations. Though these are not essential, spraying the essence mist of the angel you wish to invoke around the room and over yourself can reinforce your intent.

Take your time to raise your vibration to the highest that you can achieve. Relax completely but keep your mind focused on the angel of your choice and his qualities and abilities.

1   You will sense his presence and may see a colour or bright light in your mind. If it helps, you may mentally place an image of him before you. However, the angels rarely make themselves seen, except in the mind. The brightness of the light and love in your heart will signal his arrival.

2   Ask him what you wish to know, or state your need. Speak respectfully, but there is no need to adopt a subservient tone. Angels are understanding and loving and wish only to assist and serve.

3   You can ask questions on any subject. One particularly fruitful kind of questioning, especially when you are getting started on channelling an angel, is to ask general questions about the angels themselves. For instance:

   • Do angels evolve?
   • How can we be friends with the good angels?
   • Have angels been present since the origin of the Universe?
   • How many kinds of consciousness are there in the Universe?
   • Are there angels on other planets?
   • As a Being of Light, do you have a particular place where you reside?

4   As you begin to feel more comfortable, you can ask more personal questions, such as advice about healing, difficult relationships, and the appropriate direction for your life.

SOME ARCHANGELS AND THEIR QUALITIES

These are just a few of the Archangels you can channel:

• **Jophiel**: Helps you be faithful to a belief or cause, to overcome ignorance. Call on him for education and learning.

• **Chamuel**: Works with love, compassion and forgiveness. Call on him for help in letting go and changing old beliefs.

• **Gabriel**: For purity, order and discipline. He brings joy and grace.

• **Raphael**: Helps travellers and healers. Brings abundance, health and healing. Stands for vision and truth.

• **Uriel**: Helps people find freedom by releasing their fears and letting go of their desires.

Recognizing a Master Soul

How can you distinguish a Master Soul from others spirits who may wish to speak through you? Superior spirits are generally grouped together as a collective soul mind. In spite of this it is still possible to identify an individual Master.

Fortunately there is present-day acceptance of guides in general and knowledge through history of the many Masters who hold a higher position. This helps us to be familiar with their characteristics, behaviour and personality.

Who do we regard as a Master? Any of the biblical figures, such as a Melchizedek, Moses, Mary, Peter and many uncountable others besides, may be considered Master Souls. Some form part of a group with names such as The Ascended Masters, The Great White Brotherhood, The Celestial Sons, or Keepers of the Records. Since they do not regard one as being superior to the other, they often give a collective name to satisfy our need for an identity.

A Master guide frequently arrives spontaneously without having been invoked. Pleasure and delight accompany his arrival. The Master will present himself with the colour that is known to be his ray and that is accepted and recognized as such by the channeller. Since the Masters are Beings of Light, they only take form so that we may recognize them. It is the brightness of the light that indicates their position of elevation in the spirit world. The light is real and as bright as any electric light would be in a darkened room. It can be so bright that we only see light and no form.

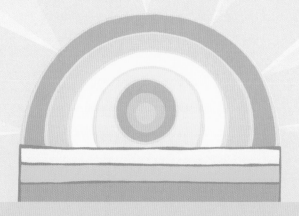

Masters use various methods of introduction. Rarely do they say their name, but they may give a feeling, an instinctive knowledge of who they are. A well-known spiritual figure from history may allow chanellers to see him as he was during his time on Earth. Moses may show himself holding the tablets, coming down the mountain, and so on. Poseidon has shown himself as Neptune. Mary brings a feeling of great compassion and gentleness.

All channellers are capable of receiving a Master Guide, but not all do so. This is because some do not feel worthy enough to have such an elevated spirit come through them. All are worthy, but because the expectation is that they cannot come, then they do not. Everyone has the Divine right to connect with the powerful loving presence of a Supreme Being.

The simplest, yet greatest test of all means of recognition is the quality and content of the message in the words. You will see the simplicity of truth and loving wisdom with each sentence. The speech will not be flowery or overabundant, but will directly address the meaning of what he wishes to say.

There is generally a strong sense of humour throughout and Masters are very good at playing with words to bring a smile when listeners become too sombre. For example, on talking about death a Master once exclaimed: 'For some it is a grave matter.'

Superior spirit Masters are more likely to speak in the manner of a philosophical and theoretical nature, rather than of a practical application of spiritual truths.

CHANNELLING A MESSAGE
FROM A MASTER SOUL

During the day or even the week before the channelling session think about the Master or Master group and the kind of information that you would find most interesting. Make some time to compose a list of questions to put to the Master. Lastly, fill your mind with what you know of the Masters, in the same way that you would want to learn all about an honoured guest beforehand if he were coming to your home. This will also help you to recognize him when he appears.

1 Once you have got over your joy at having him with you, greet him and thank him for coming. This may seem obvious, but it is often overlooked. Treat him as you would any respected visitor to your home. He will most likely ask what it is you would like to know from him.

2 Since you have prepared your questions, responding to this question should not present a problem.

3 Ask a sitter to present the questions for you if you prefer not to do the asking yourself, in case it takes you out of trance.

4 Have a glass and plenty of water handy for you to drink.

5 If the subject is spoken of at length, the Master will understand the need to keep the attention span of sitters. He will expect and encourage some interchange between them and himself.

6 He will not appreciate undue expression of adulation from the sitters when they speak to him. A respectful attitude is more suitable than a worshipful one.

7 Although he is able to speak indefinitely, you as the channeller may reach a point when you get a dry throat. This can be so bad that you are unable to continue to speak. Do not fall into the thinking that because you are channelling you cannot move or reach for a glass of water. Since you are not in deep trance you can do these things, and even open your eyes if you wish. The main reason for keeping the eyes shut is so that you are not distracted by what you see around you. With your eyes shut, your inner vision can operate more fully.

8 When you begin do not be concerned if there are pauses in which nothing more seems to be coming. Give it time, do not give up, be patient. It may simply be your soul mind interpreting before it passes on his words.

9 When the Master is fully integrated into you it can be most natural to move and gesticulate as he speaks. Your sitters will feel as if he is physically in the room and may respond accordingly.

Channelling sages

Although the experience of channelling a sage is not so very different from channelling a Master, you might especially enjoy doing so, as sages often reveal their identity as someone who is notable for his wisdom and recognized in history. However, recognizing the identity of a sage is often more for your own interest than because he wishes to be known. In addition to 'famous' sages, such as Socrates or Lao Tzu, a sage can be any spirit who has the wisdom of experience and who is learned enough to serve as a profoundly wise counsellor or philosopher. Someone who has prudence and wise foresight is also considered to be a sage.

Keep in mind that the message is more important than the messenger. However, we as human beings give more credence to one whom we recognize. The spirit world is well aware of this and, since an evolved spirit can show himself in whatever manner he chooses, he may well borrow the identity of a known sage. I say this not to demean the messenger, but to remind us that it is the message and teaching that are important.

Since a sage will almost certainly be an evolved spirit, he will have been attracted to others of similar qualities and may become part of a group. This is why it is permissible for him to present himself with a name or manner that will make the greatest impression.

We think of sages as being from ancient times and indeed there are many. They seem to come mainly from India, China or Greece. What they have said and laid down in religious teachings is often precise, profound or concerns a subject where one needs to reflect and ponder on the meaning they are trying to impart.

When one has finally understood the message, then it becomes simple and we wonder why we did not 'get it' straight away. Many of us may not readily accept the teachings because they frequently call upon us to change our ways and reflect on our lives. So often we are not prepared to do this to the degree that is required. We are urged to shake ourselves out of our stagnation and complacency.

Not all sages come from ancient times, as we do have modern wise individuals and there is no reason why we cannot channel one of these and find the language easier to understand. What is said will be more direct and less mysterious, but will carry the flavour of the ancient sages. This is because they too will have been attracted to the soul group of sages dating from earlier times.

It is important to note that in all cases what is said through you is filtered through your soul consciousness and translated according to the ability of the listeners, including yourself, to understand. The difference between the ancient and the modern way of speaking will depend on the strength of influence of the entity.

CHANNELLING A MESSAGE FROM A SAGE

It is not necessary to think or study in advance any of the teachings of a known sage, unless you want to. Remember that a sage is anyone who is wise as a result of experience, someone who acts prudently and is recognized by his contemporaries as having wise judgement. That being so, whatever message comes through and is recognizable as wisdom will be valuable to you.

However, it is not impossible for someone such as Solomon to speak to you. It is well known that he is considered wise among his other qualities. To channel a sage there needs to be within your heart a desire to benefit from wisdom and to take it seriously. A sage will not come for any less than a serious motive and will be attracted by the desire in you to learn. Not only will it be your vibration and interest that attracts a sage, but also the environment in which you live. When your home or the place where you channel is full of books on serious subject matters, including an obvious desire to know more of human nature and spiritual progression, this provides an energy or aura which is seen and recognized by the spirit world. Like attracts like.

If you can, choose a location to channel where the energy of books and practice of discourse is often present. Prepare the room as you would for any channelling session by lighting the candle and asking for the presence of the angels.

1 Relax as usual, say your prayer and ask to go to the highest vibration that it is possible for you to reach. Give yourself as much time as you need. Do not be anxious over possibly not meeting the expectations of other sitters.

2 Ask spirit to help you to interpret accurately and honestly any information that comes through. Ask that the language be simple and uncomplicated. Doing this conditions your subconscious to comply.

3 When the entity enters your energy and wishes to speak, you will know it as an urge to begin. You may hesitate and be unsure whether you really have someone with you or whether this urge comes from a desire not to keep others waiting.

4 Speak anyway. Speak about how you are feeling. Talk about any sensations you may be feeling. Voice questions on serious matters to nobody in particular.

5 A sage is happy to give advice on any subjects that concern you, including personal matters. He may prefer deep matters, but is open to assist in any way he can to give clarity. You will soon learn the right way to present a question. Here are some general questions to get you started:
   • What is the purpose of learning and study?
   • How can I attain wisdom?
   • How can I put right what I have done wrong in my life?
   • In spite of free will, do we receive any assistance when we have to make major decisions?

6 To your surprise, wise and profound answers will come in answer to your questions.

Extra-terrestrial intelligence

Many people wonder whether there is intelligent life besides ours in the Universe? Many believe that there must be. Wouldn't it be wonderful if we could communicate? Given the considerable distances and our physical inability to overcome them for reception of intelligent communication from other planets, is it not worthwhile for us to communicate from mind to mind?

There is no barrier in time or space to the consciousness of the mind. This is proven through our communications from the spirit world. For many years, channellers have reported contact with intelligent beings from other planetary systems and many books have been written about what they have to say.

It has been proposed that many of our inventions have been suggested to the mind by intelligences from beyond the Earth. Much of science-fiction writing and filmmaking about space has come to be and is now within our technology. Where did the writers get their ideas from, if not from a more advanced race? The earliest myths describe the arrival on Earth of extra-terrestrial races that altered the course of human history. There is evidence that our present culture is the result of visits of people from space.

It is clear that intelligent species have an interest in us and have, back through the ages, visited and communicated. All over the planet is evidence of that, in caves, from stories handed down and from paintings. What do they have to say to us? We have been asked again and again to love each other more. We have been asked to take responsibility for the way we treat mother Earth, or reap the consequences. We have been told that our actions now dictate how our future will be. We are told that the planet Earth is out of harmony with the other planets and that until we reach spiritual responsibility we will not be given the knowledge to travel to other areas of the cosmos using time travel instead of fossil fuels. What happens to our planet through unthinking and irresponsible action by us has an effect on the rest of the solar system.

There are many different races of planetary beings. The ones who have the most interest in us are humanoid and include some who are not dissimilar to us.

Clearly the environmental conditions have shaped how they appear, in much the same way as on our own planet there are physical differences between someone from Scandinavia and someone from the Congo, due to the climatic and geographical differences between the two areas.

We are not alone; therefore it makes sense to avail ourselves of the help that is to hand through channelling. Since the Universe is a part of the Divine Source, then it must follow that beings from space also have souls and spiritual connections. We are not so very different after all.

Why would you want to connect with an extra-terrestrial? What advantage would there be for you and others? If you agree that there is intelligent life from space that can visit our Earth, wouldn't you want to know more? You still have the option to accept or refuse what you receive during channelling. The benefit of contact and any information given through channelling is that it is a two-way street. Not only are we urged to accept and understand a being from space, but they wish to understand and experience how we feel.

Another advantage is that when an advanced being from another star system makes contact in this way he also brings with him his energy and essence, in much the same way as any other spirit being would do. For example, when you receive a Master Soul or angel you feel the energy and vibration. It is the same with an extra-terrestrial spirit. This is true whether the spirit is incarnated or not, since we are talking of mind-to-mind communication.

The essence or energy field carries with it much information, as we know from other research. When we are visited by an extra-terrestrial the vibration of his essence and energy field penetrates our own and by that means we absorb some of his knowledge and abilities.

CHANNELLING A MESSAGE FROM AN EXTRA-TERRESTRIAL (ET)

Decide that you would like to contact someone not of this Earth. It is important not to hold any fear when attempting to make contact. Fear brings what you afraid of to you, even if it is only in the mind. It is helpful to be prepared by deliberately focusing on and discussing ETs with any other sitters you may have, before you take yourself into trance. You do not want anyone to be concerned for you, should you begin to speak or act strangely.

Prepare the room. Relax as usual and say your prayer. Ask for the presence of your guardian angel. Invite any extra-terrestrial who wishes to communicate for the benefit of Earth and its peoples.

1 Hold in your mind your own idea of enlightened beings from the Pleiades, Sirius, Venus, Orion or Arcturus. There are other planets and star groups, but this will give you a start and helps you to focus on intelligent beings from space.

2 You will begin to feel a facial change. Your head will feel larger and there will be movement in your throat, as if someone is struggling to speak. The energy in the room will become stronger. It is good if the sitters say what they

are feeling and noticing in you and in the room. This will reassure you that this is not your imagining because of your desire to have something happen.

3 Your mouth may take an unusual shape as you begin to speak. The position of your mouth will make the words difficult to formulate. It might be that the communicator is having difficulty in getting the words out. Speak to him in your mind as he tries, and make

suggestions as to how the mouth should be in order to speak clearly. This will get easier each time he comes. Soon he will speak normally and give you much information.

CHANNELLING FOR OTHERS

The benefit of channelling is that it is vocalized and so can be recorded onto a tape recorder to be heard by others, whether present or not. You may have begun channelling spirit communication as an onward progression from meditation practice. This will no doubt have been in private and for your own concerns. As you begin to receive information of a more general nature and at a deeper level, you may realize that what is given is too important to keep to yourself.

With growing confidence it is likely that you have told friends of your channelling experiences. It is hard to keep such interesting and amazing experiences to yourself, isn't it? If you are part of a meditation group you will already have a ready audience of like-minded people available to you.

They may begin by asking you to put questions on their behalf when you next channel. One method of doing this is to get them to write their questions down and give them to you at the latest moment on the day you are to channel. This is so that you do not have time to put your mind to the questions in advance.

Occasionally you may channel for another when urged to do so by spirit at unexpected moments or when giving a reading. If you are surprised by a feeling that you need to go within, then do so. You will channel the information that the spirit wishes to impart.

Much more suitable is to have a group of friends sit with you while you channel. You may be nervous at first, but explain that this is the first time with others present and not to expect too much. You will then feel more relaxed. There is a first time for everything, but as you get into the relaxed altered state you will forget your nervousness.

You will meet various responses from people as you mention that you channel. Some will be interested and want to know more. Some will tell you of experiences they have had with spirit connections, which they have never told anyone before. Others will say you are crazy. When this happens do not try to convince them, but change the subject. It may be members of your family who do not want to know, or who feel uncomfortable with the idea of talking to spirit, because it is something they do not understand or condone. Simply stop talking about the subject and they will think you have dropped it and will then relax.

At some point you may be invited to channel in public. That is, before an audience, small or large. You will be concerned that nothing will come through, so prepare a speech on channelling and how it has helped you. The interest of your audience will be held and soon you will realize that it is no longer you speaking, but your guide.

He will answer questions from the audience even when they have not been voiced. This will be proved after the session when people come up and tell you this. Your spirit guide is amazing.

Public channelling

It is important that the people you invite to a channelling session are receptive to the idea of communicating with spirit minds. It helps if they are familiar with meditation and practise it themselves. Do not have anyone who is intent on debunking, who is sceptical or who will come just out of curiosity or for amusement. It is far better to have those who are genuine in their desire for spiritual advancement and further knowledge.

Be comfortable with those who come, and if possible when you first begin to have others with you restrict them to friends you know. Later, when your confidence increases, you may find that people you do not know also wish to come. If this is suggested by friends who have previously attended the sessions, ask if you can meet the new ones first. Explain to them that this is not a practice for amusement or play-acting.

Most people who would like to attend a channelling session have questions they would like to put to the entity. They hope that this contact will assist them in some way. Clearly these people would be responsible and take the evening seriously.

You are most likely to find interested parties in spiritual awareness groups or complementary healing centres. People in these places are generally interested in self-improvement and spiritual growth through connection with the spirit world. However, guard against becoming an agent for consultation on personal matters, which would not interest the rest of the group. Advise your sitters that this kind of inquiry is generally best left to a private consultation.

It is inadvisable to invite someone who is young and impressionable. Only allow a young person to attend if you have the parent's permission and are sufficiently satisfied that the youngster is mature enough and well balanced.

THE COMMON DENOMINATOR OF UNDERSTANDING

The people you invite may have already experienced channelling and so would encourage you in your efforts to channel well. It is helpful if they have open minds as to the range of entities that may appear, who belong to many dimensions beyond ours.

It is disappointing when you have contact with a Master or other evolved being, who, when inviting questions from sitters, is asked whether one should move house or not. The vibration level drops immediately, although the question is courteously answered. Spirits maintain a sense of humour, for when this happened recently they gave a picture of someone sliding down a fireman's pole. They were saying: 'Well, that has brought us down to Earth quickly.' Obviously the questioner had not recognized the elevated position of the entity or that this type of question was inappropriate. If you are channelling a guide who is close to the Earth vibration, a question of this kind is acceptable.

Invite those who sense the level of contact reached and react accordingly. The spirit communicator will always discourse at the lowest level of understanding and will not speak over the heads of those present. If you have friends who understand the importance and benefit of reaching higher superior minds and who desire to speak to them, ensure that these sitters are grouped together in one session.

THE NEGATIVE EFFECTS OF SCEPTICISM

Inevitably you will at some time have a sitter who you soon realize is very sceptical of the whole channelling scene. They may be attending simply to prove to you and themselves that it is a lot of nonsense. No matter how impressive the information and visual transformation of voice and face of the channeller, they will insist it is all a trick or just in the mind. This attitude will be obvious to the other sitters, even if he or she says nothing. It will be seen by the expression of the face and in odd comments made.

Worse than that, the energies will drop. It is probable that the sitters will be sensitive to energies, so they too will feel negative vibration coming from the sceptical person. You as the channeller will also feel the negative vibration. Your anxiety to prove your ability and to counteract this may cause a block. It is natural to be concerned when it is evident that not all are in harmony with the expectations and general belief. The clashing of ideas will also be apparent to the entity, who wishes only to enter a harmonious environment where he will be well received.

Entities at whatever level do not wish to persuade or change a person's belief, preferring them to come to their own understanding in their own time because they desire to do so. Therefore they will refrain from communicating when there is one person who does not wish to accept or believe this form of contact.

THE BENEFITS OF GOOD ENERGY

If the thoughts and energies of the group are not in sympathy with each other, this will adversely affect the overall energies of the room. Conversely when all present are in harmony, with similar intent and purpose, then the energy works well together. It is more effective to have regular group attendance composed of people who get on well with each other so that a bond forms between all of them.

Should just one member be down in health or spirits then the other people in the group will be able to assist, simply by being strong enough to add their good energies to bring about wellbeing to the one who is low. The good energy in the room, coming from positive sitters, can often bring about an improvement for any one member who has a cold or is feeling unwell.

It is easier to achieve good energies in small circle groups than in large rooms or halls. However, if you are invited to channel to a larger audience, any negative or difficult energies are usually balanced and outweighed by the larger number of positive ones.

Spirit finds it easier to enter when there is harmonious union between like-minded people. The energies are in accord and more powerful as a result. When channelling sessions are held regularly in the same room or venue, the good energies of the entities remain by penetrating the fabric of the room, including the walls. Many of you will have experienced walking into a room and sensing good and powerful energies and feeling better for it.

Setting the scene

It is important when channelling that you address a number of issues, such as the room and how it is set out; that any recording equipment is working and, if appropriate, is manned by someone responsible; and that the energy in the room is constant. If you have other sitters in the room with you, then it is also important to explain the process.

SEATING

If your channelling is held in a room rather than a hall, it should be easy to arrange the chairs so they form a semi-circle or horseshoe shape, with you at the opening head or facing the semi-circle. The chairs themselves should be comfortable, but not so much that sitters fall asleep after a while. If you have easy chairs it is best to provide cushions so that the group can sit upright and not slouch. This is so that their energies can flow easily and not be restricted through incorrect body position. Otherwise upright chairs are fine providing they will not become uncomfortable if the session is lengthy. Discomfort in the sitters will upset the energies that they send, for their minds will be focused on their need to find a comfortable position.

There will inevitably be some individuals who have more powerful energies than others. It is helpful in maintaining your own energy if you place them on either side of your seat, leaving a gap on either side of you so that they can still see you. If they are too close to you, they will not be able to monitor or see spirit overshadowing or transfiguring your form, should this happen.

The main reason for having a circle arrangement is not only so that the energy can flow round the room more easily, but also so that the sitters may see you easily from their position. Spirit is more clearly seen when it isfacing them and more difficult to see from a side view.

RECORDING EQUIPMENT

It is well worth recording all that passes during a channelling session and it is also strongly suggested that you use a good-quality tape recorder. You may be happy to have members of the group bring their own tape recorder, but it is not recommended because the clicking off when one side

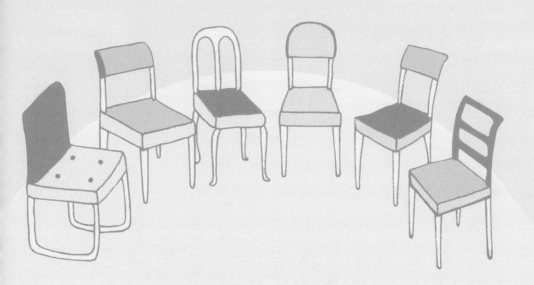

of the tape is finished will come at different times and may disturb you. The guide or entity will be aware that there is a pause in recording and this could halt the flow. This can be handled for one machine, but it is unreasonable for him to wait several times, and if he does not then there will be a loss of some of the information. What you decide to do will depend on your observation of how you and they handle having several recorders at a time, or one only.

The recording will be much enhanced if you use a lapel button mike. This will eliminate the sound of the machine interfering with the quality of the recorded material. Ask a suitable member of the group to operate the machine for you so that it is switched on when you begin, and not inappropriately when you are tuning in.

If you channel alone it is still an advantage to record what comes through. Insert an on/off switch that uses slight pressure of the fingers along the flex connecting the recorder to the electric supply. Rest the flex on your lap so that your hand is close to the switch. This cannot be done using battery-operated tape recorders.

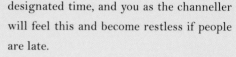

EXPLAINING THE PROCEDURE

When you have gathered together a suitable circle of people who are interested in attending your channelling sessions, the next step it to make it clear what can happen.

First of all it is important that they arrive on time are and not late. This is vital because the guides will be waiting at the

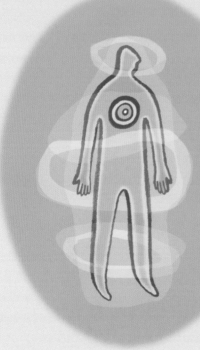

designated time, and you as the channeller will feel this and become restless if people are late.

Explain that there will be a prayer beforehand, during which all will become calm and settled to receive from spirit. Ask them to focus on any questions they have brought with them so that these are picked up by the entity.

Tell them if the session is for everyday personal or materialistic issues or to reach to the highest vibration. If you have a desire for a particular teaching or entity, tell them so that they can employ their thoughts to this end.

At times you may produce ectoplasm, which is your life force and will be seen as a white mist or vapour. You will be unaware of this happening and it is the role of the person you have allocated in the room to control the situation. It does not matter if some cough, wriggle or move in their seats, but they must not leave the room or get up for any reason. To do so would jeopardize your health, or damage you in some way.

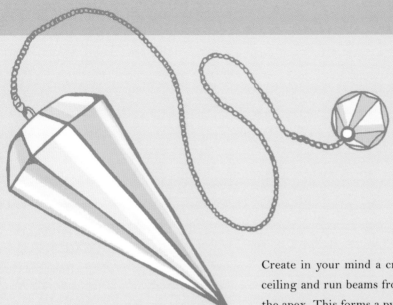

The entity will make it clear when he has finished and departs. The sitters must allow sufficient time for you to return slowly. The person who is monitoring you can, if you wish, lead chants of 'Aum' or 'Om' at the beginning and/or end of the session while you tune in and while you come back slowly to reality.

CORRECTING AND SETTING THE ENERGY

It is easy to ensure that energies are suitable for a channelling session. If they are uncomfortable or not positive, simply stand in the centre of the room, close your eyes in prayer and ask that negative energies be replaced. Imagine or place a crystal in each corner of the room. Visualize a laser beam running from one crystal to the other forming a square.

Create in your mind a crystal high in the ceiling and run beams from each corner to the apex. This forms a pyramid.

Invite the angels to come and stand in each corner of the room throughout the session. Ask for the white light of purity and protection to pour down through the apex of the pyramid and fill the room. Visualize this happening. Ask for a blessing on the evening's proceedings.

SEEKING OUT ENERGY SPOTS

Energy hot spots are common in churches, cathedrals and other places where spiritual endeavours regularly take place, or where they are on a ley line or power line. It is fortunate if you have one in the place where you wish to channel. Discover if you have by use of dowsing methods. You can use a pendulum or wire or whatever tools you find work for you. Another method is closing your eyes and moving around the room until you feel tingling or an increase in energy in your head or arms.

Preparing emotionally and physically

If you have been disturbed by upsets or disagreements between family or friends this will affect your ability to channel positive communication. It may be difficult to stop thinking of the upset, but it can be done if you are determined. Therefore if you can, put these thoughts to the back of your mind and tell your subconscious that you will deal with the problem later. None of us is immune to the upsets of daily life, but we can make the conscious decision not to allow them to interfere with our channelling work.

On the day of the session fill your mind with pleasant memories. Play music that calms you and which brings a smile to your face. Anticipate the joy you feel whenever you connect with your spirit guide or other evolved beings. In this way you will look forward to meeting once more your group and spirit friends.

During the day plan to have some time in natural surroundings because this will give you peace and bring you closer to realizing how perfect the world really is. Take a walk, do some gardening or sit by a river. Do whatever it is convenient for you to do. Find some time for day-dreaming if at all possible.

Eat lightly and try to have your main meal at midday rather than in the evening. If you do eat before the session, eat at least a couple of hours beforehand. It is best if you do not have any alcohol at all to drink during the day.

GOING INTO TRANCE WITH OTHERS PRESENT

It is best if you go into trance for the first time with friends and those who are familiar with the channelling process. At first you will feel embarrassed and worry whether anything will come through. Your friends will be understanding and sympathetic to this fear. You will soon get used to channelling in company even though you have previously channelled on your own. You will soon prefer to have others with you rather than being by yourself, since their presence adds to the energy and makes it easier.

Allocate the role of monitor and controller of the tape recorder to the person who is most experienced in channelling or mediumship.

Explain to the sitters that instead of each of them going into their own journeys as in meditation, they are to focus their thoughts on you. You will feel the difference and a big increase in energy as they do this.

Relax, go through the prayer and raise your vibration as usual. Concentrate on doing this as you do when you are alone. The concentration will help you forget there is anyone else in the room. Total focus is required.

As soon as you feel a change in you and the familiar energy of your guide, begin to speak and say what is happening. Do not wait until there is something of importance to say. He will speak when he is ready. You may tend to speak too quietly at first because of lack of confidence in yourself. Try to overcome this since it is no good if you can't be heard. Your confidence will grow as you channel in company more and more.

PRAYER FOR PROTECTION

Whatever else you do or however else you prepare for your channelling work, never neglect to say a prayer before you begin. The prayer is to protect you from any negative influences that are out in the spirit world. When you go into trance and open yourself to receive, you are not only opening yourself to the higher forces for good, but also to spirit beings whose motives are less than agreeable. The prayer is your safeguard.

Invading unwanted spirits are not necessarily bad, but can be mischievous and time-wasting. They can also deceive by adopting the identity of another.

There are earth-bound spirits who would love to enter an open door. This can be simply to make their presence known. They may have been waiting for just such an opportunity. Helping these spirits is best left to 'Soul Rescue' circles who are used to helping them to go to the Light on the other side.

Your prayer will set up an energetic spiritual force field against undesirable influences. Here is an example:

May all negative influences or thoughts, whether from without me or within me, be kept outside my connection and communication with the spirit world. May I be guided and guarded throughout and be surrounded by the light of love and truth. I ask that my guides and angels be around me to keep me safe.

You will find as you begin to say your prayer that you will immediately feel an energy increase in your head. At times this happens even when you are preparing to say the prayer and just before you begin. It is the asking that is important.

PRAYER FOR ACCURACY AND HONEST INPUT

The prayer should ask to receive accurately and honestly information given by spirit. You will inevitably wish that what you channel is interpreted accurately and does not mislead any listener. To ensure that this does not happen it is important that during your prayer you state your need to receive clearly and interpret correctly.

It is natural to want to give to others what would please and to unconsciously

adjust messages that might be less welcome. These could be instructions not to procrastinate, or not to be dominant when it would be helpful to take a back seat. While this may be good advice from spirit, you might be tempted to modify the message to make it more palatable.

You might also receive such astounding information that you wonder if you can trust your reception. Saying the prayer will reassure you that what is given by spirit is for a good reason. Here is a sample prayer to consider:

Please may I receive everything accurately and not mislead any with false information. May I always interpret messages honestly.

PRAYER AIMING FOR AND ARRIVING AT THE HIGHEST VIBRATION

Going to the highest vibration possible will give you the highest teaching in the purest and most loving way. You will be able to converse with the Masters as well as angels. Aspire to this at each session for trance. Here is an example:

Please may I go to the highest vibration that is possible for me.

Position, posture and procedure

It will be much easier to make contact with spirit and enter a trance state if you are sitting well. What does sitting well mean? First of all, make sure you have a suitable chair, if possible one where you cannot slouch. If you only have an easy chair, then have plenty of cushions to put behind your back to keep you upright.

Why upright? You wish for energy to flow easily without restriction and if you are scrunched up it has to work its way through with difficulty. It does not always succeed. Your body has energy centres called chakras, which are connected to all parts of the body. These are set in motion by the increasing energy flow drawn up from the Earth energy and, as they open more and more, they are able to connect with influences outside your physical body. This same energy as it reaches the crown chakra connects with the cosmic force and the minds of spirit. You are then united in the consciousness of all, including that of the entity who wishes to communicate with you. If you need to lie flat because of back problems or physical limitations, this is an acceptable position since you are still not scrunched up.

So here you are sitting upright and ready to go. We shall now look at the position of your arms and legs. Legs should be uncrossed so that circulation is unconstricted. Next time you are in a social meeting, notice which people are crossing their legs. Notice how many times the legs uncross and re-cross with the other leg. It is not observed by the conscious mind for it is the subconscious doing its work of keeping the circulation going. If you cross your legs during trance, they will cross and uncross several times and this action will bring your mind out of your altered state. Just when you were doing so well and getting answers, back you come to square one.

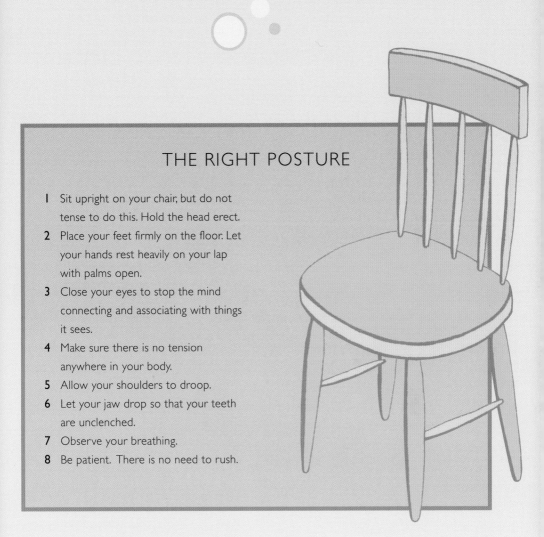

THE RIGHT POSTURE

1   Sit upright on your chair, but do not tense to do this. Hold the head erect.

2   Place your feet firmly on the floor. Let your hands rest heavily on your lap with palms open.

3   Close your eyes to stop the mind connecting and associating with things it sees.

4   Make sure there is no tension anywhere in your body.

5   Allow your shoulders to droop.

6   Let your jaw drop so that your teeth are unclenched.

7   Observe your breathing.

8   Be patient. There is no need to rush.

Folded arms indicate closing off; it is a protective defensive device. You want to be as open as possible. Put your hands in your lap with palms facing upward. Why palms up? It is not essential, but spirit beings whom you are trying to contact may sometimes place an object in your hands. If your palms are facing downward, the subconscious kicks in, knowing that nobody can hold anything that way. That thought could in turn bring you out of meditation. The sensation of having something from spirit to hold is a very real feeling and will enhance your channelling.

Answering questions from others

Receiving questions from sitters and giving answers is one of the most enjoyable aspects of channelling. It demonstrates the acceptance by your sitters of the reliability of the messages and information that come through you as a channeller. It also pleases the entity to know that there is interaction and participation with the evening's events.

Questions drive the evening along. If they are forthcoming, the entity will speak for as long as you are able to sustain his energy and for as long as they keep coming. Questions provide the opportunity for him to explain and inform on many subjects beyond the expected agenda.

Questions open the door to other worlds and widen the field of knowledge. The interaction with a higher mind stretches the minds of those who question and inquire. You may be surprised that not everybody asks questions of a spiritual nature, being more concerned with material matters and wanting spirit to

solve their problems for them. Spirit will answer, but in a manner that encourages the questioner to find their own solutions.

The phrasing of a question is very important too. Explain to the questioner that when a question is put so that there can only be a yes or no response, this limits the amount of information that could accompany a reply. Use open-ended questions such as:

- How can ——— ?
- Show me ———
- What if ——— ?
- Why does this —— ?

Ask a question so that the answers may be elaborated on. This way you will receive a teaching and not just yes or no.

The questioner does not have to be present to have a question put to the entity. You may be given the question by post, or through the hand of another. The answer will be as valid as if the questioner was with you.

Advise sitters to think in advance about what they want to ask: that is, before the session. Encourage them to ask questions of an explanatory or spiritual nature. This can be done even if the core of the question relates to a personal difficulty or decision that has to be made. For example, if there are problems between mother and daughter or other relatives, they could ask: 'Why is it that family members do not always agree?' This could lead to a discourse on karma, maturity levels, soul groups or decisions made between them all before incarnation. This one question could lead to what happens between lives, and so on.

Ask your guide to include a teaching on higher matters when a question of a lesser nature is put. Ask him to stimulate the mind further and to open up the possibilities that are there for the questioner to investigate.

You may be asked about the future. The entity will only give possible or probable futures. What is to be is dependent on actions now. To have answers to one's future in the life journey is to take away the right to choose.

How to maintain the energy and recognize when it drops

When you channel it is helpful to have your energy field operating on full power. All living beings have a body made up of vibrational energy, sometimes referred to as the magnetic field. It is through this that the entity passes information and ideas. Selfless spiritual service increases the vibrational level of the body and maintains spiritual energy by default.

The energy is channelled through the body through chakra energy centres, of which there are seven main ones. These act as miniature suns maintaining the power for your body, both physical and etheric. It will do this to varying degrees at all times. However, it is possible to increase the flow and rate of vibration in order to make contact with higher spiritual forces.

• Draw energy up from the Earth through these centres, starting at the feet.

• See this as light that grows brighter as it pushes up through the legs into the trunk. Mentally push the light of energy up through all the centres and molecules of your body.

• By the time you reach the head and crown you will be flooded with the light of strong and powerful energy.

See this energy in your mind.

• It is the mind that controls your thoughts. You may increase your energy field as far as you like by mentally expanding it into the area around you. To maintain this force field intact, visualize strengthening the outer edges.

HOW ENERGY CAN DROP

Arguments and negative people will cause all the positive psychic energy you've built up to disappear. We have all experienced being with someone who complains, criticizes and finds nothing good about life or others. Being with such a person for just half an hour can drain you and make you feel low in spirits as well.

An energy drain can also happen with those who are sick, but who in spite of this retain a positive attitude to their life. In this case their energy field is so depleted that it will draw on the stronger energy of anyone near them. It is not a deliberate conscious attempt to do this, but represents the need of the etheric body to replenish itself.

A third example is when you are near a powerfully energetic person who appears to

have more than enough energy of their own. Occasionally someone has so much energy because it is drawn off others. Again it is not a deliberate act by the person who is quite unconscious of what is happening.

In all cases simply recognize the symptoms and mentally drop a tube over you, with mirrors on the outside. This will form a barrier against energy drain. Visualize white energy pouring down through the open top of your tube and

being absorbed into your body. Remember that the mind creates a reality.

If you are channelling and the energy drops, you will feel it going. This can occur because a sitter is going off on his own journey and takes the energy from the room. Ask sitters beforehand not to journey for themselves, but to maintain focus on you. If this fails, simply ask your spirit guide to top you up with the energy that is required.

Channelling for others

There are several ways this can be done: with a group or with an individual in a private sitting, or by yourself, but for the benefit of someone who is not present. All these methods are possible for you to do while you are in a trance.

Have an easy day without any concerns that might linger and interfere with the communication to come later. Eat lightly and have nothing to drink but water for two hours beforehand.

Correct and prepare the room with good energies (see page 127), especially if you are channelling in a place that is not your own. This is even more important if channelling in a hall that has been used for a variety of functions. Lighting candles is a good practice.

Either have someone else set up the seating arrangements or, if doing it yourself, do it well in advance so that you can settle down before others arrive.

CHANNELLING FOR A GROUP

- Relax and allow yourself to go into trance. Do not be anxious if this takes time. The group understands.
- Your guide will probably begin with minor things and then invite questions from those present. If the group or audience is large, these may be varied and not all at the same level of need or spiritual awareness. Many may ask about practical materialistic matters.

- Try not to be disappointed or judgemental. Do not put your own mind to what the answer should be, but trust in the response that the entity gives.
- When it is ended, mentally thank him and bring yourself back.

CHANNELLING FOR A FRIEND OR CLIENT

When you have a one-to-one situation it is simpler. The guide has only one person to help and will probably be the individual's personal guide. He will help you know what the needs of the client are, such as information about a departed loved one.

1 Say your prayer and ask that you receive accurately and honestly.

2 It is possible a departed one will come through. If this happens, say what you see, feel or hear, even if it makes no sense at all to you. It will mean something to the inquirer.

3 When there is a situation that needs resolving, the guide knows what should be done, but will not make decisions for the client. He will guide the questioner to discover the answer for himself.

4 Since you are in a light trance only, do not be tempted to bring your own mind into play and say what you think should be done. Do not venture a negative opinion of another. Remember, guides do not pass judgement and if you find yourself doing this you will know that the channelling is not as focused as you would like. We are human and it is easy to fall into this trap. If it happens, ask your guide to come in more strongly.

5 There may be questions that invade another's privacy. The guide will not respond and will divert the question. Trust in his ability.

6 When it is over, thank him and close down the session.

Index

ACKNOWLEDGEMENTS

Executive Editor Sandra Rigby
Managing Editor Clare Churly
Executive Art Editor Sally Bond
Designer Annika Skoog for Cobalt Id
Illustrator Sandra Howgate
Production Manager Louise Hall